D0601995

Published by Periplus Editions, with editorial offices at 130 Joo Seng Road #06-01, Singapore 368357

Copyright © 2002 Periplus Editions (HK) Ltd. All rights reserved.

ISBN: 962-593-505-3
Library of Congress Card Number: 2002101487

Photo credits

All food and location photography by Luca Invernizzi Tettoni.
Additional photos by G. Molteni (endpaper) and Alan Becker (page 2).

Acknowledgments

Recipe development: Benedetta Veronelli
Text consultant: Marc Tibaldi
Translator: Natalie Danford
Coordinator: Sebastian Gutmann

Endpaper: The 13th-century Castle of the Manta (Castello della Manta) in Piedmont houses some of the most beautiful frescoes in Italy. On the walls of the great hall, a courtly dance of figures painted in the 15th century depicts important people from the region's history.

Restaurants

Ristorante Belvedere, Via Cesana, 18, 10058 Sestriere, Piedmont. Tel: (0122) 77091/76541; Fax: (0122) 76299

Trattoria I Bologna, Via Nicola Sardi 4, Rocchetta Tanaro, Asti, Piedmont. Tel: (0141) 644600

Ristorante del Cambio, Piazza Carignano, 2, 10123 Turin, Piedmont. Tel. (11) 543760; Fax (11) 535282

Ristorante Chez Pierre, Via Martorey, 73 Verrès , Valle d'Aosta. Tel: (0125) 929376; Fax: (0125) 921076

La Contea Ristorante, Piazza Cocito, 8, 12057 Neive, Piedmont. Tel: (0173) 67126; Fax: (0173) 67367

Ristorante Il Griso, Malgrate (Lecco), Via Provinciale, 51, Lombardy, Tel: (0341) 202040; Fax: (0341) 202248

Antica Osteria del Ponte, Piazza G. Negri, 9, 20081 Cassinetta di Lugagnano, Milan, Lombardy Tel: (02) 9420034; Fax: (02) 9420610

Osteria di Via Solata
Via Solata 8, Bergamo, Lombardy
Tel: (035) 271993

Distributed by

USA
Tuttle Publishing
364 Innovation Drive
North Clarendon, VT 05759-9436
Tel: (802) 773-8930
Fax: (802) 773-6993

Japan and Korea
Tuttle Publishing
Yaekari Building, 3rd Floor
5-4-12 Osaki, Shinagawa-ku
Tokyo 141 0032, Japan
Tel: (81-3) 5437-0171
Fax: (81-3) 5437-0755

Asia Pacific
Berkeley Books Pte. Ltd.
130 Joo Seng Road #06-01
Singapore 368357
Tel: (65) 6280-1330
Fax: (65) 6280-6290

First Edition
1 3 5 7 9 10 8 6 4 2
09 08 07 06 05 04 03 02
PRINTED IN SINGAPORE

THE FOOD OF
NORTH ITALY

Authentic Recipes from Piedmont, Lombardy, and Valle d'Aosta

By Luigi Veronelli
Photography by Luca Invernizzi Tettoni

Featuring recipes from the following restaurants:

Ristorante Belvedere   La Contea Ristorante
Trattoria I Bologna   Ristorante Il Griso
Ristorante del Cambio   Antica Osteria del Ponte
Ristorante Chez Pierre   Osteria di via Solata

PERIPLUS

Contents

Part One: Food in North Italy

*Not only is the northwest Italy's fashion capital,
it also boasts the nation's finest wines, truffles, mushrooms, and game*

The visitor expecting spaghetti with tomato sauce and pizza will hardly recognize northwestern Italy as being Italian at all. This area—comprising the regions of Piedmont, Lombardy, and Valle d'Aosta—nestles in the Alps bordering Switzerland and France, and its cuisine might be confused with that of its neighbors. In fact, the North is somewhat aloof from the rest of Italy and every few years there are rumblings about it seceding from the poorer south though no one takes this seriously.

North Italy will also surprise the traveler who thinks of Italians as laid-back and relaxed, who imagines them taking long afternoon naps after leisurely lunches. Piedmont is the home of several enormous corporations—including Fiat, Italy's largest car manufacturer, responsible for 37 percent of the country's gross national product—and offers a luxurious sophistication perhaps more often associated with France than with Italy. Turin, in particular, and Piedmont are generally known for lush, gilded cafés, artistic pastries and chocolates, and truffles—one of the world's most expensive foods. Nevertheless, the region is still surprisingly agricultural, and also produces Italy's finest wines, as well as several kinds of nuts and the usual rich Italian array of produce.

Lombardy, with its capital, Milan, is Italy's fashion, business, and banking center. Although the countryside of Lombardy is still heavily agricultural, the region boasts a cuisine that can hardly be considered rustic, even in the most rural areas, dependent as it is on butter, cream, rice, and cheese. Lombardy's is a culinary tradition rich not only in history, but also in calories. It is also a highly varied tradition, with each town offering its own particular specialty.

Valle d'Aosta is often overlooked in studies of Italy because of its minuscule size, but to do so is a mistake. Landlocked Valle d'Aosta is home to several famous peaks—Mont Blanc, Mount Rosa, the Matterhorn, and the Gran Paradiso (which at 13,324 feet is the centerpiece of Italy's largest national park)—but few people. With 115,000 inhabitants, it is the least populous of Italy's regions. Valle d'Aosta has no large cities; its capital, Aosta, has only about 37,000 inhabitants. The food is hearty and surprising. Ingredients like cabbage, cheese, and the local dark rye bread sustain the region's inhabitants over long Alpine winters. As in all of northwestern Italy, there is no sign of tomato sauce anywhere here—just inventive food made with high-quality ingredients. Ultimately, that is what makes food Italian.

Opposite:
Established in 1757, Ristorante del Cambio—Turin's most famous restaurant—is located on Piazza Carignano, overlooking the Palazzo Carignano. It was traditionally a meeting place for the aristocracy and important political and cultural figures of the kingdom of Piedmont.

A Land of Riches

*The wide selection of fine produce found in northwestern Italy
translates into some of the tastiest dishes in Italian cuisine*

From remote mountain villages and sprawling vineyards to some of the world's most sophisticated cities, the northwest of Italy—Piedmont (Piemonte), Lombardy (Lombardia), and Valle d'Aosta—offers a great study in contrasts. And it is not only the landscapes that are varied, but this area also boasts both sophisticated city-styled culinary traditions and rustic farmhouse cooking. As in all of Italy, climate and agriculture create each region's culinary destiny here; the inhabitants of these three provinces and their subdivisions eat fine, locally grown produce.

Thanks to the Po River—Italy's largest—there is no problem growing produce in abundance in the northwest. The Po River originates in northwest Italy, at Mount Monviso in the Cottian Alps, and runs through Turin and then eastward along the southern border of Lombardy until it empties into the Adriatic. Not only does the Po effectively cut off this region from the rest of the country; it also creates some of the most fertile farmland in Italy. The river's valley is an ideal growing environment, and the river itself and its tributaries supply abundant water.

This part of the country is dairy territory. In the countryside, cows and goats provide milk, much of which is used to produce the outstanding cheeses for which northwestern Italy is famous. Milk appears as an ingredient in soups and rice dishes in all three of these regions, and anyone convinced that the "Mediterranean diet" relies only on olive oil will be shocked to see the copious amounts of butter used in most dishes here.

Likewise, anyone convinced that Italians eat pasta every day will be surprised to see the range of inventive *primi*, or first courses, served in this northwest corner of the country. Fresh egg pasta is common, but more often northwestern Italians begin a meal with a soup, rice-based dish, or polenta.

The Piedmont diet in particular relies heavily on rice. Rice has grown in the flood plain of the

Opposite:
Together, Piedmont and Lombardy produce the most amount of wine in Italy.

Left:
Rice has been grown in the Po Valley since the 15th century.

Piedmont is a large producer of cheese, the most famous types being bra, tome, tomini, castelmagno, acceglio, *and* bross.

characteristic—its creamy and soupy consistency.

The people of Piedmont and Lombardy have a reputation in Italy for working hard and for living lavishly. Lombardy is home to Italy's famous fashion houses, while Piedmont is historically linked with a house of a different type: the House of Savoy, Italy's former royal family, which after 1861 ruled almost all of what is today modern Italy.

Both Lombardy and Piedmont have as their centerpieces bustling and large (at least by Italian standards) cities: Turin in Piedmont and Milan in Lombardy. Each of these is in turn surrounded by charming smaller cities, such as Asti, Alba, and Vercelli in Piedmont; and Cremona, Pavia, and Mantua in Lombardy.

Valle d'Aosta is a bit of an outsider among this cosmopolitan group. It is Italy's smallest and least populous region with 115,000 inhabitants. Although sparsely inhabited, Valle d'Aosta is home to several mountains—Mont Blanc, Mount Rosa, the Matterhorn, and the Gran Paradiso (which at 13,324 feet is the centerpiece of Italy's largest national park). Its capital, Aosta, is certainly not a city on the level of Milan and Turin.

Where Valle d'Aosta does keep up with its flashy neighbors, however, is in its agriculture and cheese production. While Lombardy produces a vast number of different types of cheese, Valle d'Aosta concentrates on one: Fontina. In this tiny region, Fontina is carefully regulated and codified, and locals are able to determine the season—perhaps even the month—in which the cow provided the milk that went into a specific cheese's production. Fontina is made from whole

Po Valley since 1475. Most likely it was imported from Spain, where it had been introduced by the Arabs. Today the Piedmont town of Vercelli is the location of the national rice market. The rice grown in this area is medium- to short-grain rice, such as *arborio*, *vialone nano*, and *carnaroli*, and all three of these have a special starchy coating. This coating is released during the cooking of *risotto* to provide the dish's most marked unpasteurized milk of one milking. It is then pressed, scalded and ripened. Fontina has a delicate nutty aroma and a smooth, slightly elastic texture with some small round holes.

Valle d'Aosta has numerous orchards and is famed for its pears and apples—particularly the small and flavorful rennet apples. It is also a major honey producer. Chestnut-flavored honey is a typical Valle d'Aosta product, and chestnuts are used in many ways in this region. They are still ground into flour that is used to thicken soup as well as to make sweet and savory tarts.

As is true of all of Italy, the northwest has been conquered and dominated many times over the millennia. Piedmont was dominated by the Romans, the Franks, and the Lombards over the years until it came almost completely under the rule of the House of Savoy, along with Sardinia, after 1400. When Italy was still a series of city-states, the impulse to unite into a single country in the 1800s (a project that did not reach completion until 1861) was led by Piedmont.

Valle d'Aosta was originally a Roman settlement created to provide a barrier between Rome and the bellicose Gauls. The first inhabitants of this region were the Salassi, who lived in Valle d'Aosta more than 2,500 years ago. They were succeeded by the Romans (who conquered the Salassi and sold them as slaves). The Romans recognized the importance of centrally located Aosta and made it their base. When the Roman Empire fell, Valle d'Aosta came under the rule of the church. It is a relatively young region, formed only in 1945.

Lombardy was Celtic from the 5th century BC until it was conquered by Rome in 201 BC. After several centuries of attack by barbarians, it became the kingdom of the Lombards, a Germanic people, in AD 568. The Lombards lost control of the area to King Charlemagne in 774, but the region still bears their name.

While the days when Italy's city-states fought each other and invading forces are over, there is one subject that still raises the hackles of Italians from any region: the suggestion that their foods might not be superior to all others. While the foods of these three regions might seem mighty similar to an outsider, rest assured that, if questioned about the best food in Italy, or even in the world, their inhabitants will answer with certainty that the best food in the world is found in their backyards, and chances are they won't be speaking metaphorically.

Also called cèpes, *porcini mushrooms are pale brown in color and can weigh from 1 oz (30 g) up to 1 lb (500 g); their caps range from 1 to 10 inches in diameter. Porcini have a smooth, meaty texture and pungent, woody flavor.*

The Cuisine of Lombardy

*The gastronomic variety in Lombardy
is as exciting and diverse as the region itself*

Although Lombardy's capital, Milan, is its best-known city—Milan has been important both politically and economically for more than ten centuries and is famous for dishes such as *risotto alla milanese* and *costoletta alla Milanese*—the region's other cities and provinces each have their own charms and culinary specialties.

Cremona is as renowned for its piquant mustard as for its finely crafted violins. Pavia is home to one of Italy's best universities and is known for its *magro*, or meatless dishes. Brescia and Bergamo boast the gilded look of small, wealthy cities and serve equally brilliant yellow dishes of polenta. Mantua offers a Renaissance cooking style that derives from the famous Court of the Gonzagas—spices and sweet-and-sour combinations are prevalent.

The lake district of Lombardy, home to Lakes Como, Maggiore, and Garda, is a beautifully groomed vacation area where fabulous freshwater fish is served, and frog's legs are a surprisingly common ingredient. And the northern part of Lombardy, the Valtellina, is an alpine haven with fabulous food such as *pizzoccheri* (buckwheat pasta) and *bresaola* (air-dried beef) and wines. Indeed, Lombardy houses perhaps the widest range of cooking styles of any region in Italy, hence resulting in food that is as exciting and diverse as the region itself.

One area in which Lombardy's diversity is truly astounding is cheese. Some of Italy's best cheeses are made in Lombardy, and the region produces an overwhelming number of different types.

Grana Lodigiana is seasoned for one to two years and fashioned into large cylinders weighing from 50 to 80 pounds (24 to 40 kilograms). It has a hard, golden yellow crust and is traditionally eaten both as a table cheese and grated.

Lombardy is also home to creamy Mascarpone, a snow-white to straw-colored substance that is more cream than cheese. Mascarpone is, in fact, coagulated cream aged just 24 hours. It is often eaten on its own, but is also an important ingredient in tiramisù and other dishes. *Stracchino*, which today basically refers to Crescenza but also includes Taleggio, Gorgonzola, and some *robiola* cheeses under its etymological umbrella, is slightly acidic and has no crust. It is milk-white and can be spread like butter. Strongly-scented Taleggio, on the other hand, has a soft texture and delicious taste, and it is a full, rich cheese and slightly sweet. Spicy Gorgonzola, is marbled with the green mold that gives it its unmistakable aroma; it hails from a town of the same name.

Other cow's milk cheeses include compact and strongly flavored Bagoss from the Bagolini

Opposite:
The Imperialino restaurant at the Grand Hotel Imperiale, Moltasio, by Lake Como.

mountains of Brescia with its hint of bitter herbs from the mountain pasture. Bagoss is eaten as a table cheese after two months ripening or allowed to mature up to six months for a more piquant, harder cheese that is used for grating. Bitto hails from the mountains of Gerola and, traditionally, contains one-fifth goats' milk. It is eaten either as a table cheese or, after ripening for up to three years, as a hard, grating cheese. The flavor of Bitto displays a hint of hazelnuts. Branzi of Bergamo is sweet when young but grows increasingly aromatic and spicy as it ages. The *robiola* cheeses of Valsassina are semi-hard and fall somewhere between sweet and spicy on the flavor scale. A reddish-brown rind that develops after the cheese has ripened for several weeks characterizes *robiola*.

In addition to its wide selection of cheeses, Lombardy offers many cold cuts, including bresaola—salted, dried, and lightly smoked beef filet. *Berna* is sheep's meat dried in the sun at 2000 meters (Tonale is famous for it). *Busecchin* is a blood sausage found throughout the southern Milan area. Coppa is a kind of salami made from the upper neck of a pig (Pietragavina is the main source). Cotechino sausage is made with spiced ground pork rind and pork thigh. Cuz is young lamb cooked and preserved in its own fat, typical of Val Camonica.

Monza's *luganega* pork sausage is excellent both on its own and in risotto. Mortara is the place to go for goose salami, Mantua and Cremona for cooked pork salami. And finally, Valchiavenna and Compodolcino prepare *violino*, a goat—or occasionally sheep—thigh brined with herbs and spices and then dried and smoked.

No midday Italian meal is complete without a *primo*, or first course, but while in the rest of Italy that usually indicates a pasta dish, Lombardy has stretched the definition of *primi* to include polenta (which may also serve as a side dish) and all types of *risotto*. Pasta appears here, too, of course, mostly in the form of *casonsei* and *tortelli*. These are both stuffed pastas, the first filled with various types of meat, and the second available in numerous versions, including those with meat, cheese, or vegetables.

Different varieties of cheese, served at the Il Griso restaurant in Lecco.

Food is tied to age-old traditions throughout Italy, but in Lombardy some of the most ancient cooking methods are still in use. The Lombards—the Germanic people who ruled Lombardy from 568 to 774, and lent their name to the region—introduced clay cooking there in the 6th century. This method is still used in Valcuvia, most commonly with pheasant. The bird is seasoned, wrapped in clay, then placed in an oven. When the clay shell cracks all the way around, the dish is cooked. The clay is then shattered, and the meat eaten at its fragrant best.

However, the Lombardy oven is more commonly used for making the region's famed cakes and other sweets than it is for clay cooking. The best known Lombardy cake is *panettone* (see right). This sweet yeast bread with citron, candied orange peel, and sultanas is traditionally prepared at Christmas time and is now eaten throughout Italy. There are various myths surrounding the origins of its name: one claims that it derives from *pan de Toni*, or "Toni's bread," supporting the theory that a baker named Toni was the first to make it. It may also come from pan de ton, or "fancy bread." *Colomba pasquale* is another seasonal treat—this one associated with Easter—that originated in Lombardy but is now enjoyed throughout Italy. *Colomba pasquale* means "Easter dove," and this cake is baked in a special bird-shaped pan.

Lombardy has much more to satisfy a sweet tooth. *Bussolano* is a typical Mantua doughnut; *cannoli* and *tortina* come from Lodi; Carnevale offers *chiacchiere*. There are *fave dei morti*, *offelle* from Parona, and *oss de mord* (literally, "bones of the dead"). *Pan de mein* is eaten with cream on Saint

Along with the Duomo and Teatro alla Scala, Cova's panettone—the finest example of this typical Lombardy Christmas cake—is a symbol of Milan.

George's day. Bergamo has sweet polenta, while both Mantua and Cremona lay claim to *sbrisolona* (the Mantua version contains almonds, while the Cremona version is rich with walnuts). Finally there are also the almond cakes of Pavia, Cremona's *torrone*, and *torta di latte*. In short, Lombardy's sweets are as varied and tempting as all its foods, and provide a most luxurious ending to any fabulous meal in the region.

Sophisticated Milan

The capital city of Lombardy
offers high-brow dining in exquisite surroundings

The capital city of Lombardy, the financial capital of Italy and the fashion capital of the world, Milan cannot help but impress. It is home to Leonardo da Vinci's "The Last Supper" and home base for fashion houses like Armani and Versace, as well as furniture designers like Ettore Sottsass, and its architecture ranges from the neoclassical La Scala opera house to the Baroque Palazzo di Brera dating back to 1651.

The city's culinary landmarks are just as fascinating. People from all over the world come to Milan, and it is one of the few places in Italy where you will find exotic foreign restaurants offering the foods of countries in Asia, Africa, and the Americas. Because natives of other regions have also migrated to Milan, you will find restaurants representing those cuisines as well. Milanese cooking is interesting in its own right, however—it is as sophisticated and creative as its birthplace.

Milan boasts two dishes that bear its name and that are very closely associated with the city. First, there is *risotto alla milanese*, a beautiful saffron-tinged rice dish. The (possibly apocryphal) story of its origins involves another of Milan's symbols: the city's Duomo, an imposing Gothic structure that seems to cast its shadow over the entire metropolis. From 1572 until 1576 the Flemish painter Valerio da Perfundavalle worked on the stained-glass windows of the Milan Duomo, and he used a pinch of saffron, diluted in water, to enrich the yellows in his palette. The apprentice assigned to handle saffron duties came to be nicknamed Zafferano, or Saffron. In 1574, Zafferano married the boss's daughter, and they held their wedding banquet in the cloister behind the Duomo's apse. As a practical joke, the groom's friends added saffron to the rice. Wedding guests relished the dish, and it quickly grew popular throughout Milan. Today it is accompanied by *ossobuco*, a slow-cooked veal shank served with a long-handled spoon so that the diner may scoop out the bone marrow as a final treat.

After centuries of refinement, the classic version of *risotto alla milanese* calls for rice to be toasted lightly in sautéed butter, onion, and bone marrow, then brought to a boil with saffron-flavored beef broth. The *risotto* is then removed from the heat and butter and Grana cheese are stirred in. Carlo Emilio Gadda (1893-1973), the Milanese author who wrote, among other books, *That Awful Mess on Via Merulana* and *Acquainted With Grief*, had this to say about his native city's most famous dish: "Risotto alla Milanese should never be overcooked, please, no! It should be slightly more than *al dente* on the plate. The grains should be soaked and swollen in their

Opposite:
The most well-known restaurant in Milan—the Savini restaurant.

juices, with each grain an individual, neither stuck to its companions, nor resting soggy in sludge, which would be unpleasant. Expert *risotto*-makers allow just a touch of grated Parmesan. This dish is worthy of the serious and elegant people of Milan."

Milan's other culinary star is *costoletta alla Milanese*, or breaded veal cutlet. When properly cooked, it is crisp on the outside, but juicy on the inside. While this may seem like an exceedingly simple dish for such a complex city, but it represents an interesting aspect of Milan: the foreign rule in its past.

Over the past two millennia or so, Lombardy has been under the thumb of a variety of groups—everyone from the Franks to the French have conquered this valuable territory, and since Milan has existed as an important city since Roman times, it usually served as headquarters for these invaders. Lombardy, and as a result, Milan, was under Austrian rule from 1814 until 1859, and Milanese cuisine still bears the stamp of Austrian influence, not least of all in *costoletta alla milanese*, which is basically Vienna's beloved *wiener schnitzel*.

Actually, the Milanese believe that it was not their city that adopted the veal cutlet from Vienna, but the other way around. In fact, Austrian commander Joseph Radetzky—governor of the Austrian kingdom of Lombardy-Venetia from 1850 to 1857—sent a missive to the Court of the Hapsburgs that supports this claim. In it, he described Milanese cuisine and mentioned one particularly delicious item: a veal cutlet dipped in egg, then in breadcrumbs, and cooked in butter. While this was a side note to Radetzky's report, it reportedly struck a chord with the emperor, and upon his return to Vienna, Radetzky was summoned to the court to instruct the head cook there in exactly how to recreate this delicacy.

Another Milanese dish, *cassoeula* (a name that derives from the Castilian *cazuela*) is instead a legacy of Spanish rule. In 1540, Hapsburg Emperor Charles V invested his son, soon to become Philip II of Spain, with the local duchy. Spanish rule stayed in place until 1706. This dish has countless variations, but the most common adds sausage, pancetta, and goose gizzard to a base of cabbage, pork rind, pig's feet, and other pork products. *Cassoeula* is served with bread or polenta.

A Milanese dish that has spread throughout the world is *minestrone*, which literally means "big soup." This is a soup of beans, vegetables, and pasta or rice. Ingredients will vary depending on the season and a particular cook's recipe, but *minestrone* is always hearty and satisfying.

Finally, because Milan is a city on the go, it has more than the average share of *paninoteche* or sandwich shops. These feature Lombardy's famous cheeses, as well as all sorts of cured meats and vegetables. One terrific place to find fresh sandwiches—and just about anything else—is Peck, an enormous food hall in downtown Milan. In addition to sandwiches, Peck offers delicious baked goods, roasted meats, cheeses, wine, and truffles. It is the place to stock up for a picnic or a homemade gourmet meal. A visit to Peck ranks as one of the great Milanese experiences—like the city in which it is located, this beautifully presented shop is alluring, sophisticated, and expensive.

Opposite:
Not only is Milan the fashion capital of the world but the city also boasts some very chic eateries.

Alpine Kingdom

*From the mountains to the plains, Piedmont and Valle d'Aosta
are rich in natural beauty, fine wines, and exotic foods*

From the mountains to the plains, Piedmont and Valle d'Aosta are rich in natural beauty, fine wines, and exotic foods. Both these regions offer cuisines that lean more to those of neighboring countries than to those of their countrymen. With its dependence on butter, wine, and dairy products, Piedmont's rich and strong regional style is more reminiscent of French cooking than Italian, and Valle d'Aosta's reverence for potatoes and cheese definitely lends its food a Swiss flavor. However you categorize the foods of these two regions, one thing is certain: they are delicious.

Wine connoisseurs believe that wherever great wines are made, a great cuisine inevitably develops alongside them. This is certainly the case in Piedmont, homeland to the best red wines in Italy, as well as many excellent whites. Not only is wine enjoyed as a beverage here, but it also appears as an ingredient in many dishes. For example, while in other parts of northern Italy *risotto* is generally cooked with white wine, here it is often tinged pink with a local red, resulting in a much more robust flavor.

And *risotto* is featured frequently on the Piedmont table, even though it is a rather new arrival in Piedmont. Until just a few decades ago, most rice was boiled in beef or vegetable broth and then drained and added to the final dishes. Today, rice is used not only in *risotto*, but also in soups, side dishes, salads, stuffings, and even in a few desserts. Typical dishes include *riso alla piemontese*, or Piedmontese-style rice, with or without truffles, *riso alla canavesana*, *paniscia* (rice with beans), *brodera*, and *ris in cagnon*.

Despite this ongoing infatuation with rice, Piedmont also has a strong egg pasta tradition. The two most common forms of egg pasta here are *tajarin* egg noodles (they would be called *tagliatelle* elsewhere in Italy) and *agnolotti*, half-moon shaped ravioli stuffed with greens and a touch of meat.

Take milk and cheese away from the Piedmont kitchen, and you would hardly eat at all. Milk is used to make soups, soften roasts, prepare desserts, and

Left:
One of the most famous grappa *distilleries in Italy is that of Romano Levi who has been distilling the spirit in Neive since 1945.*

balance spicy, strongly flavored dishes such as hare (*civet*). Cheese is another key ingredient. The various types of cheeses have their own specific and strong personalities, beginning with *bra*, a semi-fat, raw, hard cow's milk cheese. *Tomini* are small cheeses with mixed milk types; *tome* is made with whole milk and has a spreadable texture; *castelmagno* is semi-fat and hard, with a distinctive marbled appearance; *acceglio* is a fresh cheese; and extraordinary *bross* cheese is finished with a soak in milk or *grappa* and white wine.

Both Piedmont and Valle d'Aosta preserve old communal dining traditions that require diners to gather together around a single pot. Perhaps these traditions developed as a way to stay warm in the harsh Alpine winters, or perhaps they were simply invented to make dining fun. *Bagna caoda*, a classic Piedmont dish, is one such collective meal. Anchovies, garlic, oil, and butter are melted together and serve as a hot dip (the name *bagna caoda* literally means "hot bath") for a variety of winter vegetables. One of the joys of *bagna caoda* is the ritual of eating it. Diners gather around and dip their vegetables into a communal pot, which is balanced over a small burner, called a *s'cionfeta*.

When it comes to sweets, Turin rules Piedmontese

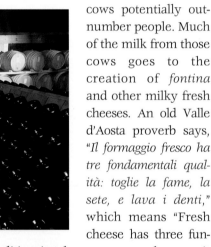

Racks of Spumante bottles are cellared twenty meters below ground at Piedmont wine producer Fontanafreddo.

cuisine. As early as 1600, the art of working with cacao was so well-developed in this city that Swiss chocolate makers came to Turin to work as apprentices. The chocolates with hazelnut known as *giandujotti* (because they resemble the hat that Gianduia, a Turin Carnival figure, wears) are native to Turin. The *diablotin*, *givo*, and *alpini* created by Turin's confectioners are equally tasty.

Piedmont may be known for its cosmopolitan pleasures, but Valle d'Aosta is a region of peaceful mountain lanscapes—one of those areas in which cows potentially outnumber people. Much of the milk from those cows goes to the creation of *fontina* and other milky fresh cheeses. An old Valle d'Aosta proverb says, "*Il formaggio fresco ha tre fondamentali qualità: toglie la fame, la sete, e lava i denti,*" which means "Fresh cheese has three fundamental qualities: it takes away your hunger, it quenches your thirst and it brushes your teeth."

Cheese in general is crucial to the cooking of the Valle d'Aosta, but it is Fontina that is the region's lifeblood. Fontina has been made in Valle d'Aosta for at least 700 years; 7.7 million pounds are produced yearly. One of the many ways in which it is put to good use in Valle d'Aosta is in *fonduta*, or fondue. As with the *bagna caoda* of Piedmont, diners share a communal pot.

Perhaps because of the cold weather, hearty soups are the most common *primi*. These include all types of vegetable soups, usually with cheese and bread included. Chestnut soup is a seasonal treat.

Other first courses include polenta or gnocchi with melted cheese. Potatoes are eaten not just in gnocchi, but boiled or roasted as side dishes.

Main dishes often feature local game such as venison and chamois: Valle d'Aosta has a long and valiant hunting tradition, not least of all because the House of Savoy, the Italian royal family, had its hunting grounds there.

The area's most famous entrée is *carbonada*, a salted rump steak slow-cooked with onions, butter, bacon, cinnamon, and wine and served over polenta. *Cotoletta alla valdostana* is a fried veal cutlet topped with *prosciutto* and *fontina*. *Boudin*, or blood sausage, also appears frequently. Cured products include mocetta, a leg of veal, chamois or goat, and *prosciutto di* San Marcel, prepared with eighteen different herbs.

As if its wine tradition could never flourish in the shadow of the wildly successful vineyards of Piedmont, Valle d'Aosta has never developed well-known labels. (It does have this distinction

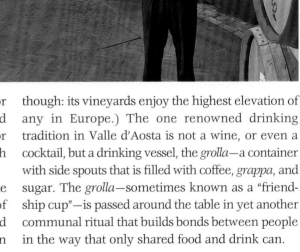

Fontanafreddo, one the largest and most historic producers of wine in Piedmont, makes Barolo, Spumante, and a range of local Alba DOC wines.

though: its vineyards enjoy the highest elevation of any in Europe.) The one renowned drinking tradition in Valle d'Aosta is not a wine, or even a cocktail, but a drinking vessel, the *grolla*—a container with side spouts that is filled with coffee, *grappa*, and sugar. The *grolla*—sometimes known as a "friendship cup"—is passed around the table in yet another communal ritual that builds bonds between people in the way that only shared food and drink can.

White Gold

The celebrated white truffles of Alba

Even among the many breathtaking landscapes in Piedmont, the serene Langhe area stands out in terms of visual beauty. Neither Alpine nor Apennine; it falls between southern Piedmont and northern Liguria. The Langhe is an area of green hills dotted with ancient trees and meadows of flowers. The Langhe is not only exhilarating visually, however—it is a standout in gastronomic terms as well. When it comes to the area's most prized culinary gem, however, visual beauty is not a part of the equation. The white truffle—also known as the Alba truffle—is an ugly gray knob, one of those foodstuffs that makes one wonder who was the first brave soul to attempt eating it. Yet its flavor is fabulous—earthy and alluring, yeasty with a slight hint of mold. There is quite simply nothing to compare to its highly particular aroma and marked flavor.

Though not particularly sightly, truffles possess an exquisite flavor that is venerated the world over.

The white truffle is a hypogeous fungus shaped like a tuber that lives in symbiosis with trees (oaks, hornbeams, hazelnut trees, ilexes, poplars, and others). It has a smooth or rough peel that is off-white or gray in color. Its flesh is brown with white marbling, and its strong scent is extremely enticing. White truffles vary in size—a single knob can weigh more than one kilogram. Over the years, many myths have developed around white truffles: they are rumored both to be aphrodisiacs and to spur those inhaling their aroma to predict the future. More prosaically, white truffles also aid digestion. They are eaten raw, either sliced thinly or grated and sprinkled over first and second course dishes just before serving. White truffles do need at least some fat to draw out their flavor. If you were to take a bite out of a raw truffle as if you were eating an apple, you would surely be disappointed, but contact with a small amount of fat releases the truffle's fabulous aroma and flavor. (Black truffles have a dark outer layer and a lighter inside. They are found mainly in Tuscany and Umbria and are cooked rather than served raw.)

Truffle hunting is a time-consuming and difficult exercise, which explains the high price of these culinary prizes. During certain periods, truffles are literally worth their weight in gold. Traditionally, dogs—often mixed breeds—assist humans in locating truffles. Truffle hunting takes place during the night or at dawn, when dogs' olfactory powers are more sensitive due to the cooler air. As soon as a properly trained dog smells a truffle, it begins to dig. The dog's human companion then steps in and retrieves the truffle. An expert truffle hunter carefully detaches any ripe specimens, then covers the hole and makes a note of its location in order to return to gather the rest as they ripen.

When purchasing truffles, look for firm ones with a strong smell. Clean with a soft kitchen brush or cloth, much as you would a common mushroom. They only keep for a week or so. To get the most out of truffles, many people store them in a bed of rice, or even with a few fresh eggs. The eggs or rice absorb some truffle flavor, without depleting its supply.

White truffle season runs from October through early January, and during that time the cooks of the Langhe seek perfection while preserving, rediscovering, and reworking ancient and traditional truffle recipes. The usual Piedmontese suspects—*agnolotti, tagliatelle, bagna caoda*, enormous platters of mixed boiled meats, fondue, and hare—may all be served with a wonderfully scented blanket of truffles. Strictly local specialties include a salad of foraged mushrooms sliced extremely thinly and dressed with anchovies, oil, and lemon and then covered with truffles, and beef braised in Barolo, rabbit with peppers, and walnut tart. These dishes can be tasted in the best restaurants, or experienced in small, unknown trattorie located in the towns and villages spread out over the hills of the Langhe.

The Truffle Fair in Alba takes place every year in the fall and is the only place to be for afficionados of truffles.

Truffle madness reaches its peak each year in the fall when the Fiera del Tartufo, or Truffle Fair, takes place in Alba. This exposition, which has been an annual event since 1929 and is an offshoot of turn-of-the-century harvest celebrations that took place in the Langhe, draws tens of thousands of tourists from Europe and even farther afield. The fair involves theater productions, art exhibitions, concerts, and of course many tastings and meals.

Dining and Drinking in North Italy

From coffee bars to fine restaurants, Northwest Italy is a gourmet's paradise

It's an old pop anthropology law that each culture invents a rich vocabulary for the items that are central to it. So just as the people of Alaska are rumored to have numerous words for snow, Italians have a wide range of terms to refer to eateries. There are *ristoranti* (restaurants), *trattorie* (more casual eateries), *osterie* (even more casual, akin to taverns), *enoteche* (wine bars), and *caffè*, not to mention specialists such as *pizzerie*, *paninoteche*, *gelaterie*, and *birrerie*.

Piedmont has no lack of any of these establishments, but its *enoteche* and *caffè* deserve special mention. Piedmont is perhaps Italy's top wine-producing region, bearing as it does the grapes for 37 different DOC (*denominazione di origine controllata*) wines and four DOCG wines. This is the homeland of grapes such as Barbera, Nebbiolo (a key component in Barolo and Barbaresco, among other wines), and Dolcetto. While many Italian wines are intended to be consumed young, Piedmont makes several that are intended to be aged—perhaps due to the influence of neighboring France, where aging is the norm. *Enoteche* are popular in Piedmont. They often serve salty snacks along with wine. The region's wine producers hold tastings as well. And if your taste runs to fortified wines, try a vermouth in Turin, where it was invented in 1786.

Despite this bounty of wine, Turin's most famous drink has to be coffee. Turin is Italy's buzzing coffee capital—perhaps its strong industrial backbone is fueled by caffeine. This is headquarters for Lavazza, Italy's largest coffee roaster. (Lavazza even runs a "coffee school" in the city, with classes on roasting, grinding, and tasting.) No surprise, then, that Turin's main thoroughfares are lined with sparkling caffès, one more swank and inviting than the next, and many dating back to the 19th century—some even farther. Caffè Confetteria al Bicerin is Turin's oldest continuously operating establisment and has been in business since 1763.

Along with fabulous coffee, many caffès offer the city's much admired chocolates. Modern European chocolate originated in Turin—it was here that chocolate was first formed into bars and squares meant to be consumed out of hand. Today the city hosts the annual Eurochocolate festival. Gianduia is Turin's signature chocolate: a blend of chocolate and finely ground hazelnuts. It is formed into small candies called *gianduiotti*.

Elsewhere in Piedmont, in the Langhe area and particularly in the city of Alba, during truffle season, and for a price, restaurateurs will top almost any dish with shaved truffles, which fill the area's dining rooms with their intense scent. Among these

Opposite:
Tonino, the founder of La Contea, Neive, stands at the door of his wine shop-cum-bar, which stocks more than 700 varieties of wine and grappa from Piedmont, Alba, and the rest of Italy.

are Belvedere in La Morra (Cuneo province), which also boasts an interesting wine museum. La Contea, in the town of Neive in the same area is a well-regarded restaurant serving classic Piedmont cuisine. Here you will find an impeccable version of *bagna caoda*, for example.

Not to be outdone by its neighbor to the west, Lombardy, too, is home to some of Italy's finest and most elegant restaurants, not just in Milan, but throughout the region. One phenomenon that is common throughout Italy is even more pronounced here: restaurants serve home-style food, perhaps gussied up to fine dining standards. Generally speaking, with the exception of the few "ethnic" restaurants popping up in Italy (mostly Chinese, except in Milan, which is somewhat more international) when Italians eat out, they eat the same dishes they would eat at home. This is true regionally as well—a restaurant in Lombardy will rarely serve food from Sicily. So while a home-based meal in Lombardy might consist of a simple *minestrone* (one Lombardy dish that is now known all over the world) made with odds and ends found around the house—a handful of beans, a few leaves of spinach—the *minestrone alla milanese* at Osteria di Via Solata in Bergamo contains *pancetta*, eleven different kinds of vegetables, and a generous topping of herbs and cheese. In Lugagnano, just outside of Milan, you will find Milanese classics such as *risotto alla milanese* and *costolette di vitello alla milanese* on the menu of Antica Osteria del Ponte di Cassinetta.

Lombardy is Italy's top cheesemaking region, and—particularly in the northern Valtellina area—you can visit many small cheesemaking operations and taste their products, much as you might go on a wine-tasting expedition in an area with a large number of wineries. Cheese often appears as its own course on menus in Lombardy, as well as popping up as an ingredient in dishes such as *pizzoccheri* (buckwheat noodles with cheese and cabbage).

Italians also adhere strictly to eating locally when it comes to meat dishes versus fish dishes. In the lake region, most restaurants specialize in fish from the lakes. At Ristorante Il Griso in Malgrate, you will find fish from nearby Lake Lecco on the menu. Il Cantuccio is another excellent choice in the lake district—it is located in the Como province.

Finally, charming Valle d'Aosta does not have a tradition of fancy restaurants at all. Instead, it is dotted with eateries serving more rustic fare, such as Chez Pierre in Verrès, which serves traditional local foods like cabbage soup. Fondue is quite common in Valle d'Aosta's restaurants.

While Piedmont and Lombardy have several large cities apiece, Valle d'Aosta is still a more rural region. Because its inhabitants are more closely tied to the land, the arrival of seasonal ingredients is always marked here, both by special festivals devoted to individual foodstuffs (salami, *fontina* cheese, and even lard) and by changes to restaurant menus so that the freshest items are always featured.

While the coffee of Valle d'Aosta is not as celebrated as the coffee of Piedmont, it does have its own special character—namely that it is generously spiked with *grappa* and sugar and served in a *grolla* or communal drinking cup with several spouts. This is a decidedly convivial way of ending a meal, whether in someone's home or in a restaurant.

Opposite:
Romano Levi is probably the most lucid example of a grappa *distiller who not only makes a world-class spirit, but who also paints his own bottle labels by hand.*

Part Two: The North Italian Kitchen

The secret to delicious North Italian cuisine
lies in sourcing fresh ingredients from quality producers

As with most Italian cuisine, the food of North Italy does not require many complicated techniques; it is a straightforward food that relies instead on the natural flavors of fresh produce. North Italian cooking uses a variety of common cooking methods, such as grilling, sautéing, boiling, and roasting. And cooking North Italian dishes is not difficult for the average home cook since the equipment used is the same as that which is found in any modern kitchen.

Sourcing quality ingredients is recommended, start off with fresh flavors and the battle is half won. Shop around for a good olive oil, grana cheese, and a suitable rice for making *risotto*. Apart from frying fish, when a light vegetable oil is often preferred, good quality extra virgin olive oil is essential for drizzling over salads or for use in cooked dishes.

Quality Parmigiano-Reggiano cheese is a must; avoid packaged grated "parmesan" which is simply not a viable substitute for serious cooks. Buy smaller quantities of the cheese as it may dry out.

When cooking *risotto*, an Italian rice such as *arborio*, *carnaroli*, or *vialone nano* is required.

Most important of all, however, is access to fresh vegetables and quality meat. The food of North Italy is simple to master as long as you cook with good quality, fresh and flavorful basic ingredients.

Making Polenta

Traditionally, polenta is prepared in a large copper pot known as a *paiolo*, but any type of large pan will suffice. Although the cooking time here may seem excessive, don't try and skimp on it. You will end up with undercooked polenta that is bitter and hard to digest.

Rock salt to taste
6 cups (1½ liters) water
1 lb (500 g) cornmeal for polenta

In a large pot, bring generously salted water to a boil. As soon as it begins to boil, add the cornmeal very slowly in a thin stream, stirring continuoulsy with a wooden spoon. Continue stirring constantly, and in the same direction, until the polenta is extremely thick (stirring should be difficult) and can be pulled away from the sides of the pan, about 45 to 60 minutes. Serve the polenta warm, or pour onto a wooden board to cool. Cooled polenta may be cut into slices, which can then be toasted, fried, or grilled.

Opposite:
For a soft and creamy polenta, look for finely ground cornmeal, for a more unrefined, chewy polenta, use coarsely ground cornmeal.

North Italian Ingredients

A list of common and unusual products
found in every well-stocked North Italian pantry

Artichokes

Arugula

Borlotti (left) and
cannellini beansBroccoli

ALCHERMES: A red Italian liqueur made from alcohol, sugar, rose water, orange peel and vanilla, with various spices such as cinnamon, coriander, cloves, aniseed flowers, and cardamon; the cochineal gives it a bright red color. In Florence it was widely used at the time of the Medici who were great Admirers appreciating it not only as a liqueur to drink but also as a preparation in many sweet dishes. Today, the use of alchermes is very limited but it is still enjoyed in the preparation of some traditional desserts. If unavailable, substiute with Marsala.

AMARETTO COOKIES: These almond flavored cookies, similar to macaroons, are used in many dessert recipes. Readily available from quality bakeries and supermarkets.

ARUGULA: The flavor and texture of this tasty green, also known as rocket, changes drastically over its lifespan. Young arugula leaves are soft and mild; more mature leaves are tougher and sharper, to the point of being peppery. When using arugula in salad, look for young, bright green leaves.

ARTICHOKE: A member of the thistle family, and one of the most Italian of all vegetables. There a dozens of varieties and countless ways of preparing them. See also Cardoon.

AUBERGINE: See Eggplant.

BAY LEAF: Indigenous to the Mediterranean region, bay leaves have been used since classical times, not only as a flavorant for food but also to make the laurels with which classical warriors and athletes were corwned. A common constituent of bouquet garnis, court bouillons, and marinades.

BORLOTTI BEANS: These small beans, sometimes labeled cranberry beans or Roman beans, are pink and beige and usually available in dried form. They are similar in flavor to kidney beans.

BROCCOLI: In addition to the green heading broccoli, Italians grow sprouting broccoli producing numerous small heads over a long season. The chartreuse romanesco is popular, as are the more common purple and white varieties. In fact, the Italians often refer to romanesco broccoli as cauliflower.

CALF'S LIVER: When purchasing liver, look for a shiny surface. Use any liver you do buy within twenty-four hours, as it doesn't keep well. If your butcher hasn't removed the membrane on the outer surface of the liver, do so before cooking.

CALF'S LUNG: Lung needs to be cooked at length in order to be edible. Ask your butcher to supply the lung already chopped.

CAPER: Pickled flowers of the caper bush. They are sold preserved in brine, vinegat or salt and should be wahed before use.

CARDOON: A close relative of the artichoke and very similar in taste and appearance to a globe artichoke. The stalks and roots are tender and delicious when steamed. See also Artichoke.

CARROT: Choose bright orange, shiny carrots; avoid those with cracks or which are limp. Baby carrots with their green tops still intact do not require peeling and are particularly flavorful.

CHESTNUT: Wild chestnuts are common in Italy. Polenta was first made using chestnut meal before the introduction of maize from the New World. Chestnut meal is now used in the production of various flat cakes and as a thickener.

CORNICHON: A kind of small gherkin. If cornichons are not available, use regular cocktail gherkins.

COTECHINO SAUSAGE: Cotechino is a traditional sausage made with pork rind, lean pork meat, and back fat. The coarse mixture is seasoned with cloves and cinnamon and formed in a pig's casing. It must be cooked before eating.

COURGETTE: See Zucchini.

EGGPLANT: Choose eggplants that are not too large but which are firm, with smooth, shiny skins and bright green stems. Also known as aubergine.

EGGS: 2 oz (60 g) eggs in all the recipes in this book.

FENNEL: Fennel is one of the most popular vegetables in Italy. The bulb is often just braised, and drizzled with olive oil, and sprinkled with bits of anchovy or Parmesan cheese. It is frequently used in salads or as an *antipasto*. Fennel leaves are also used to flavor salads, sauces, soups, and stews.

FONTINA VALDOSTANA: Made from whole unpasteurized cow's milk of one milking, Fontina from Valle d'Aosta is a semi-soft cheese with a delicate, nutty flavor (similar to but sweeter than Gruyere.) As is melts easily, and fairly evenly, is good for cooking. The best wheels of Fontina, which can weigh as much as 40 lb (18 kg), are made between May and September in the mountain chalets of the region.

GRANA CHEESE: Grana cheese is a large category of hard, dry cheeses that includes Parmesan cheese and Grana Padano cheese. These types of cheese are usually grated and sprinkled over pasta just before serving, or brought to the table so that each diner can serve him- or herself. Purchase chunks of such cheeses and grate them yourself, just before using. Pre-grated cheese dries out and loses much of its flavor.

GRAPPA: A dry, transparent, high-percentage alcohol made by distilling grape skins and vines that is usually consumed in small amounts after a meal. It is also used as an ingredient in some dishes. Grappa is available in most liquor stores.

JERUSALEM ARTICHOKE: Rather confusingly, this plant has nothing to do with Jerusalem or artichokes. It is actually from North America and is a relative of the sunflower, which is from Peru. (It is thought that the word Jerusalem is a corruption of *"girasole,"* the Italian name for sunflower.) The Jerusalem artichoke was introduced into Europe in the early seventeenth century and it is the tuber part of the plant that is eaten. This knobbly tuber can be boiled, fried or eaten raw.

Broccoli

Cardoon

Chestnut

Eggplant

fennel

Flat-leafed parsley

Marjoram

Porcini

JUNIPER BERRY: These purple-black berries are often used in stews and game dishes. Crush the berries lightly with the back of a knife to release their flavor before cooking.

MARJORAM: This herb, which is somewhat similar to fresh oregano, seems to brighten up just about any dish. Marjoram has tiny leaves, which should be removed from its tougher stems. Do not substitute dried marjoram for fresh.

MARSALA: This dark, sweet wine is almost syrupy in consistency. It adds depth to all kinds of desserts and some savory dishes as well.

NUTMEG: Dried nutmeg lasts almost indefinitely and is useful to have on hand to shave into various sweet and savory dishes for flavor.

OLIVE OIL: Use extra-virgin and virgin olive oils for simple, uncooked dishes and for salads, otherwise any quality olive oil will suffice for the recipes in this book. When deep-frying, use pure olive oil or groundnut (peanut) oil.

OREGANO: A somewhat confusing term which is commonly used to represent a particular herb but which in fact is a name representing many herbs of the marjoram family as well as others.

PANCETTA: Pancetta is often compared to American bacon, although it is not smoked. Pancetta is rolled up into a cylinder and then cured. It is sold in slices—usually thinner than slices of prosciutto or salami. Some recipes simply will not taste the same without the savory addition of a little pancetta, so make an effort to find the real thing at Italian specialty stores.

PARMESAN: The most famous of the Grana cheeses. See Grana.

PARSLEY: Flat-leafed parsley—the variety used in North Italy—is the most popular herb in European cookery. The stems and leaves are chopped up to use as a flavoring or as a garnish. Curly-leafed parsley possesses a slightly different flavor and is more commonly used as a garnish only.

POLENTA: Ground cornmeal is cooked into mush, then eaten either warm and soft or cooled and cut into slices (that may then be grilled). Look for imported Italian polenta in specialty stores. Steer clear of instant polenta.

PORCINI MUSHROOMS: Fresh porcini mushrooms are thick and meaty and have a strong aroma. Do not confuse them with dried porcini mushrooms, which are flavorful once rehydrated but cannot be used in salads as the fresh mushrooms can.

PROSECCO: This *spumante*, or sparkling wine, is the most frequently consumed in Italy. Prosecco on its own stands as a perfect aperitif, though it may also be served with fish, cheese, and white meat.

RICOTTA: In North Italy, ricotta is often smoked, and in Piedmont it is sometimes mixed with paprika.

RISOTTO RICE: *Risotto* is a creamy rice dish made with certain kinds of Italian rice. The most common types of *risotto* rice are *arborio* rice, *carnaroli* rice, and *vialone nano* rice. All have short, stubby grains and cook to a satisfying, firm consistency.

ROSEMARY: A shrub native to the Mediterranean area, rosemary leaves are highly aromatic and are commonly used in Italy to flavor marinades, meat, and poultry dishes.

SAFFRON: Orange stigmas of a type of crocus, they are very expensive and only a few threads are used in each recipe.

SAGE: A member of the mint family, sage is a common herb in Italy and the best sage in the world is considered to come from the Dalmatia, on the Adriatic coast. Once a medicinal herb, sage is now used as a flavoring in Italian cooking, usually for slightly more robust dishes.

SAVOY CABBAGE: The cabbage most often used in Italy is Savoy cabbage, a variety with curly leaves and a slightly more delicate flavor than common green cabbage, which is also acceptable. Look for firm, tight heads. Avoid any yellow-looking cabbage. Fresh cabbage smells sweet and mild; the sulfurous odor many people associate with cabbage indicates that it is no longer fresh.

SCALLION: Also known as spring onions, scallions (used as a garnish or flavor enhancer) are sometimes treated as a vegetable in their own right and served as an appetizer or as a side dish.

SPRING ONION: See Scallion.

THYME: This herb works particularly well with all kinds of Mediterranean flavors. Fresh thyme leaves are green, but sometimes have a gray tint to them. A single sprig of thyme will have many small leaves. Sprigs of thyme are often used whole (sometimes as part of a bouquet garni), then removed before serving.

TRIPE: There are two kinds of tripe (which is part of a cow's stomach): smooth tripe, which has a smooth surface, and honeycomb tripe, which has a waffled appearance. Honeycomb tripe is generally more flavorful and tender. In Italy, tripe is soaked in lime, brined, and then boiled before it reaches the shelves, which reduces the cooking time considerably. If you purchase tripe that has not been prepared in advance, it will have to be boiled before being used in the following recipes.

TRUFFLE: Fresh truffles are very expensive but only a tiny amount is used in each recipe. As well as the famous white truffles of Alba, North Italy also boasts black truffles from Piedmont.

VINEGAR: Many kinds of vinegar exist but the most common types used in Italian cookery are wine vinegars and balsamic veingar. Wine vingegars are somtimes flavored with herbs and are widely available from supermarkets. Balsamic vinegar, which originates from Italy, is made from grape must, which is reduced by slow simmering and is then fermented for a year before being aged in barrels. Factory-produced balsamic vinegar is much quicker to produce but does not posess the same qualities as that made in the traditional style. Look for a quality balsamic vinegar.

ZUCCHINI: These green vegetables are at their best in the spring. Look for firm-fleshed zucchini (courgettes) that haven't been punctured. Female zucchini are sometimes sold with their yellow flowers still attached. These are completely edible and make a lovely garnish.

Rosemary

Savoy cabbage

Scallion

Zucchini

Part Three: The Recipes

Basic recipes for pasta dough, sauces, and purées precede those for the main recipes, which begin on page 40

Buckwheat Pasta Dough

Prepare this pasta dough for Pizzoccheri (page 64).

2 cups (280 g) finely ground buckwheat flour, sifted
$^2/_3$ cup (85 g) all-purpose (plain) flour, sifted
4 eggs
1 tablespoon lukewarm water, or as needed

Combine both flours. On a large wooden cutting board or pasta board, shape the flour mixture into a well. Crack the eggs in the center, add water, and beat lightly with a finger. Draw in a small amount of flour from the side of the well and mix with the eggs until you have a paste.

Move the remaining flour from the well on top of the dough and knead to incorporate. If dough is sticky, sprinkle on additional flour, or if dough is too dry add a little additional water. Knead by hand until the dough is consistent, smooth and moist, but not sticky or gummy, about 10 minutes. Shape the pasta dough into a ball and set aside to rest for 20 minutes. Scrape the work surface clean.

Flour work surface lightly and return dough to floured work surface. Use your hands to flatten the ball slightly, then roll out the dough, turning it a quarter turn in between each roll. Complete a final thinning of the pasta by wrapping about one-third of it around the rolling pin and rapidly

Measurements

Measurements in this book are given in volume as far as possible: 1 measuring **cup** contains 250 ml (roughly 8 oz); 1 **teaspoon** contains 5 ml, while 1 **tablespoon** contains 15 ml or the equivalent of 3 teaspoons. Australian readers please note that the standard Australian measuring spoon is larger, containing 20 ml or 4 teaspoons, so use only $^3/_4$ tablespoon when following the recipes.

Time Estimates

Time estimates are for preparation only and do not include actual cooking time.

  🕐 *quick and very easy to prepare*

  🕐🕐 *relatively easy; less than 15 minutes' preparation*

  🕐🕐🕐 *takes over 15 minutes to prepare*

Servings

All recipes serve 4 unless otherwise stated.

Established in Turin in 1915 by Antonio Peyrano, the family-owned and operated chocolate producer makes some of the best chocolates in Italy. Peyrano's insists on only using local Piemontese hazelnuts in its chocolates.

rolling back and forth. This dough should be slightly thicker than the dough for regular egg pasta. Cut the sheet of dough into noodles that are $\frac{1}{2}$ in (1 cm) wide and $2\frac{1}{2}$ in (6 cm) long.

Pasta Sheets

Prepare this pasta dough for Stuffed Pasta (page 58), Frog Leg Ravioli (page 56), and Bergamo-style Stuffed Pasta (page 54).

> $3\frac{1}{2}$ **cups (440 g) all-purpose (plain) flour,**
>   **sifted**
> **4 eggs**
> **Pinch salt**
> **1 teaspoon extra-virgin olive oil, extra**

To make the pasta, on a large wooden cutting board or pasta board, shape the flour into a well. Crack the eggs in the center along with a pinch of salt and olive oil and beat lightly with a finger. Draw in a small amount of flour from the side of the well and mix with the eggs until you have a paste.

Move the remaining flour from the well on top of the dough and knead to incorporate. If dough is sticky, sprinkle on additional flour. Knead by hand until the dough is consistent, smooth and moist, but not sticky or gummy, about 10 minutes. While kneading, flour your hands occasionally. When done, shape the pasta dough into a ball and set aside in a lightly floured bowl, covered with plastic wrap and set aside to rest for 30 minutes. Scrape the work surface clean.

Flour work surface lightly and return dough to lightly floured work surface. Divide dough into 2 balls and with lightly floured hands, flatten each ball slightly. Roll out one of the balls with a lightly floured rolling pin, turning it a quarter turn in between each roll. When the dough is $\frac{1}{8}$ in thick, complete a final thinning of the pasta by wrapping about one-third of it around the rolling pin and rapidly rolling back and forth until it is very thin and even, about 8 x $10\frac{1}{2}$ in (20 x 26 cm). Repeat with remaining ball.

Egg Ravioli Dough

Prepare this pasta dough for the Truffled Egg Ravioli (page 60).

> $2\frac{1}{2}$ **cups (275 g) all-purpose (plain) flour,**
>   **sifted**
> **3 eggs**

On a large wooden cutting board or pasta board, shape the flour into a well. Crack the eggs in the center and beat lightly with a finger. Draw in a small amount of flour from the side of the well and mix with the eggs until you have a paste.

Move the remaining flour from the well on top of the dough and knead to incorporate. If dough is sticky, sprinkle on additional flour. Knead by hand until the dough is consistent, smooth and moist, but not sticky or gummy, about 10 minutes. While kneading, flour your hands occasionally.

When done, shape the pasta dough into a ball and set aside in a lightly floured bowl, covered with a lightly floured clean dish towel. Scrape the work surface clean.

Watercress Purée

Prepare this purée for the Frog Leg Ravioli (page 56).

3³/₄ oz (115 g) watercress, washed well

Bring a large pot of salted water to a boil, add watercress and cook for 2 minutes or until bright green. Refresh in cold water and squeeze out as much water as possible. Pass through a food mill or process in a food processor to form a thick purée.

Conserva Casalinga di Pomodoro
Tomato Purée (La Contea)

Small amounts of tomato purée are called for in numerous Italian recipes.

This is an excellent example and can be used to make a wonderful plain tomato sauce for pasta.

20 lb (10 kg) tomatoes
2 lb (1 kg) onions, chopped
2 carrots, chopped
¹/₂ rib celery, chopped
1 lb (500 g) bell peppers (capsicums), halved, seeded and diced
3¹/₂ oz (100 g) garlic
¹/₄ cup basil
¹/₄ cup parsley
¹/₄ cup rosemary
1 cup (125 ml) extra-virgin olive oil
Salt to taste

In a large pot, cook the tomatoes over high heat until they give up their liquid.

Pour off the cooking liquid from the tomatoes and combine it, in another large pot, with the onions, carrots, celery, bell peppers, garlic, basil, parsley, and rosemary. Cook over low heat, stirring frequently, for 1 hour.

Purée both tomatoes and cooked vegetables through a food mill.

In another large pot, heat the oil over medium heat. Add the tomato and vegetable purées. Season to taste with salt. Bring to a boil, then turn down and simmer 20 minutes, stirring frequently.

While the purée is still warm, pour it into sterilized jars and allow to cool. Hermetically seal the jars and preserve their contents, following sanitary canning methods. Makes 6 lb (3 kg) purée.

Rattatuia di Verdure
Ratatouille (La Contea)

This dish will only be as good as the quality of the vegetables used to make it, so substitute what is in season in your area.

If you use eggplant (aubergine), bell peppers (capsicum), cauliflower, and cardoons, replace the lard with salt-preserved anchovies that have been soaked and then mashed into a paste. This can be served over pasta (*tagliatelle* and *maltagliati* are both good choices) or as a side dish.

2 tablespoons extra-virgin olive oil
1 teaspoon minced lard
6 small zucchini (courgettes), chopped
4 scallions (spring onions), white and green, chopped
4 heads spring garlic, white and green, chopped
12 fava (broad) beans, peeled if mature
¹/₄ cup freshly shelled peas
2 tablespoons minced marjoram

2 tablespoons minced oregano
2 tablespoons minced thyme
2 tablespoons minced rosemary
2 tablespoons minced parsley
Salt to taste
$^1/_4$ cup (60 ml) beef broth, warm
6 zucchini (courgetts) flowers, cut into strips
1 tablespoon tomato purée
15 basil leaves

In a large pan, heat the olive oil. Add the lard and cook until just golden. Add the zucchini, onions, garlic, fava beans, peas, and minced herbs. Season to taste with salt. Cook, stirring occasionally, until flavors have combined.

Add the warm beef broth and cook an additional 3 minutes.

Add the zucchini flowers and tomato purée, and tear the basil leaves directly into the pan. Cook for 1 minute. Serves 4.

Fried Semolina Squares

Prepare fried semolina squares to accompany Mixed Organ Meats (page 104).

$^3/_4$ cup (180 ml) milk
2 tablespoons sugar
4 tablespoons semolina flour
1 egg yolk
3 tablespoons all-purpose (plain) flour
1 egg, beaten
$^1/_4$ cup (10 g) breadcrumbs

Lightly oil a mold for the semolina mixture and set aside. Place milk in a saucepan over medium heat and bring to a boil. Add the sugar and semolina flour and cook for 10 to 15 minutes, stirring constantly. Remove the saucepan from the heat, cool slightly, then stir in the egg yolk. Pour into the oiled mold and allow to cool completely. Unmold semolina mixture and cut into $^2/_3$-in ($1^1/_2$-cm) cubes. Coat first in flour, then in beaten egg, and then in breadcrumbs, pressing slightly to make them stick. Set aside.

When ready to serve, fry the semolina squares in the oil and drain on absorbent paper. Remove to a warm serving platter.

Pan di Spagna • *Sponge Cake*

This plain cake forms the basis for several Italia desserts, but it is also tasty on its own, with a simple sauce, or coated in jam or pastry cream.

$^3/_4$ cup (95 g) all-purpose (plain) flour
Extra flour for coating pans
$^2/_3$ cup (100 g) potato starch
8 eggs
Pinch salt
$1^1/_4$ cups (315 g) white sugar
$3^1/_2$ tablespoons butter, melted
Extra butter for buttering pans

Preheat oven to 350˚F (180˚C, gas mark 4). Sift flour and potato starch together and set aside. Line the bases of two $6^1/_2$ x 8 in (16 x $19^1/_2$ cm) loaf pans. Butter and lightly flour the sides of each loaf pan.

Fill a medium saucepan with enough water so that the base of a large bowl placed on top just touches the surface of the water. Place over high heat, bring to the boil, then reduce heat to medium. Meanwhile, place the eggs and salt into the large bowl and whisk until combined. Add the sugar and continue to whisk for 3 to 4 minutes or until all the sugar has dissolved.

Place the bowl over the pan of hot water and whisk constantly until the mixture just starts to thicken and become light in colour, taking care not to let the egg mixture start to cook.

Turn off heat and continue whisking for 10 to 15 minutes or until the mixture becomes cold and thick enough that the trail of a whisk lightly dragged through the mixture holds its shape for 1 minute.

Sprinkle half of the flour mixture over the top and carefully fold into mixture until almost combined. Sprinkle with remaining flour mixture and carefully fold into mixture until just combined. Pour over melted butter and gently fold in to incorporate.

Pour the batter into the prepared loaf pans and bake until firm, 20 to 25 minutes.

Remove pans from oven and allow cakes to cool slightly in their pans before unmolding onto a wire rack. Allow to cool completely. Makes 2 cakes.

Cheese Sauce

This cheese sauce-cum-fondue must be started the night before the meal and can be served with Cardoon and Jerusalem Artichoke Flan (page 74).

$6^2/_3$ oz (200 g) Fontina Valdostana cheese, rind removed and cubed
$2^3/_4$ cups (700 ml) milk
1 egg yolk
1 tablespoon butter

In a large saucepan, combine the cheese and $^1/_2$ cup (125 ml) of the milk; cover with a tight-fitting lid, and set aside overnight in a cool place.

If serving with Cardoon and Jerusalem Artichoke Flan, prepare the flan first then finish the sauce just before serving.

Place saucepan over very low heat and stir constantly with a wooden spoon for 10 to 15 minutes or until cheese has melted and the mixture is creamy. Add the egg yolk stirring to combine. The mixture should remain smooth and creamy. Add the remaining 1 tablespoon butter and stir until melted and combined.

"BAGNA CAODA"

Vegetables with Anchovy Sauce (La Contea)

This is one of Piedmont's most famous dishes, and though it may seem exceedingly simple, the results are spectacular. *Bagna caoda* was originally peasant food but it now appears on the most chic tables. Appropriate vegetables include cardoons, broccoli, cauliflower, endive, escarole, small onions, leeks, Jerusalem artichokes, cooked or raw white turnips, roasted beets, slices of fried squash, boiled potatoes (skin on), roasted onions, and yellow and red bell peppers (capsicum). ⏀

10 cloves garlic
$^3/_4$ cup (190 ml) extra-virgin olive oil
5 canned anchovies in oil, $^1/_2$ oz (15 g), drained
Raw vegetables of your choice, julienned or cut into bite-sized pieces

Crush 3 of the cloves of garlic and thinly slice the remaining 7 cloves. Place oil and sliced and crushed garlic in a small pot over very low heat. As soon as the garlic colors slightly, add the anchovies. Stir to dissolve.

Transfer the small pot to a burner on the table in an arrangement similar to a fondue pot. Serve vegetables and allow each diner to dip vegetables into the anchovy dip. Serves 4 to 6.

PEPERONATA

Sweet Pepper Stew (La Contea)

This very simple stew combines the sweet flavors of bell peppers (capsicum) and tomatoes, and can be served either as a side dish or as an appertizer on its own or on bruschetta. The tastiest bell peppers in Italy originate from an area strecthing from Voghera in southern Lombardy to Asti in southern Piedmont. ⏲

2 tablespoons extra-virgin olive oil
1 tablespoon butter
1 medium red onions, chopped into
    $^1/_2$-in (1-cm) pieces
2 large red bell peppers (capsicums),
    chopped into $^1/_2$-in (1-cm) pieces
2 large green bell peppers (capsicums),
    chopped into $^1/_2$-in (1-cm) pieces
2 large yellow bell peppers (capsicums),
    chopped into $^1/_2$-in (1-cm) pieces
1 clove garlic, minced
3 ripe plum tomatoes, cored, seeded and
    chopped into $^1/_2$-in (1-cm) pieces
Salt and pepper, to taste

Heat the oil and butter in a large skillet over medium heat. Add the onions and peppers and cook for 4 minutes. Stir in the minced garlic, cook for 30 seconds, then add the tomatoes. Simmer 5 minutes until thickened. Remove from heat and season to taste with salt and pepper. Serves 4 to 6.

INSALATA CON QUAGLIE

Quail Salad ((Trattoria I Bologna)

Use a mix of your favorite lettuce leaves for this tasty salad of grilled quail breasts. Frisee lettuce, savoy cabbage, and arugula would be ideal here. ⏱

8 quail breasts
Salt
Freshly ground black pepper
3 tablespoons extra-virgin olive oil
1 tablespoon white wine vinegar
4 teaspoons fresh herbs such as chives, tarragon, and parsley, finely chopped
8 boiled quail eggs, halved
6 cherry tomatoes, quartered
1 oz (30 g) truffle, thinly sliced
4 dried porcini mushrooms, soaked in water
2 cups salad leaves of your choice such as frisee lettuce, savoy cabbage, and arugula
Few sprigs fresh Italian parsley, to garnish

Season the quail breasts with salt and pepper and coat in 1 tablespoon of the olive oil. Broil (grill) or pan-fry them over high heat for 2 minutes each side or until cooked; set aside.

Prepare the herb dressing by combining the remaining olive oil, vinegar, and herbs, then add salt and pepper to taste.

Divide the salad leaves, eggs, tomatoes, mushrooms, and truffle slices between four plates then pour on the dressing. Cut each quail breast in half and place 4 on each plate. Garnish with fresh parsley. Serve immediately.

MINESTRONE ALLA MILANESE

Milanese Minestrone (Osteria di via Solata)

In the summer you may pour *minestrone* into soup bowls after it is cooked and allow it to cool before serving. It may also be topped with slices of lean *pancetta* that have been cooked in the *minestrone* itself. In Lodigiano, the cheese is added to the soup just before it finishes cooking. ② ②

7 tablespoons butter
1 small onion, finely chopped
1 small leek, finely chopped
1²/₃ oz (50 g) *pancetta*, blanched and chopped
1 bouquet garni of 3 parsley sprigs, 1 rosemary
    sprig, and 1 bay leaf
1¹/₂ teaspoons salt, or to taste
¹/₂ teaspoon freshly ground black pepper
1 small potato, peeled and cubed
1 medium zucchini (courgette), thinly sliced
1 small carrot, cubed
1 small celery heart, white finely chopped
¹/₄ head Savoy cabbage, about 1 lb (500 g),
    thinly sliced
¹/₂ cup (80 g) shelled fresh peas
³/₄ cup (190 g) canned tomato purée
15-oz (445-g) can *borlotti* beans
8 cups (2 liters) beef broth
¹/₂ cup (115 g) Vialone rice
2 tablespoons finely chopped basil
2 tablespoons finely chopped parsley
3 cloves finely chopped garlic
1 tablespoon finely chopped fresh bay leaf,
    optional
¹/₄ cup (30 g) grated Grana cheese, or to taste

Heat a medium saucepan over medium heat and add 1 tablespoon of the butter. When melted, add onions, leek, blanched *pancetta*, and the bouquet garni. Cook until the onions are transparent, about 4 to 5 minutes. Discard the bouquet garni. Season to taste with salt and pepper.

Meanwhile, heat a large saucepan over medium heat and add remaining the 6 tablespoons of butter. When melted, add potatoes, zucchini, carrots, celery, cabbage, and peas and cook for 10 minutes, stirring constantly. Add the onion mixture, tomato purée, salt, pepper, and *borlotti* beans and cook for a further 2 minutes, stirring constantly. Add beef broth and cook for 3 minutes or until vegetables are cooked *al dente*.

Increase heat to high and add rice. Stir and cook for 8 minutes. Add the minced basil, parsley, garlic, and bay leaf and continue cooking until the rice is cooked, about 5 to 8 minutes.

Remove soup from heat and let it rest for about 5 minutes. Transfer soup to a tureen and serve immediately. Garnish with grated cheese if desired.

Serves 4 to 6.

ZUPPA ALLA VALDOSTANA

Cabbage Soup (Chez Pierre)

This hearty dish is halfway between a soup and a casserole. Don't make this with canned broth—it just won't have the same flavor. ☺ ☺

3 lb (1½ kg) beef shoulder
8 cups (2 liters) cold water
1 medium carrot, roughly cubed
1 medium onion, unpeeled and cut into
    8 equal pieces
1 small leek, cut in half
1 rib celery, leaf and stems cut in half
4 black peppercorns
1 tablespoon rock salt
½ head Savoy cabbage, about 1⅔ lb (800 g)
2 tablespoons butter
1 lb (500 g) packet thinly sliced black bread
3 cups (375 g) thinly sliced Fontina Valdostana
    cheese
1 teaspoon ground cinnamon

Place beef in a large saucepan with the cold water, adding more water if necessary so that beef is just covered. Place over high heat and bring to a boil, carefully skimming foam. Add carrot, onion, leek, celery, black peppercorns, and rock salt, return to the boil, then reduce heat and simmer for 2 hours, skimming foam occasionally. If necessary, add a cup or so of boiling water during this time so that meat is just covered with liquid.

Remove from heat and skim fat from surface. Remove meat from cooking liquid and reserve for another use. Strain broth and reserve vegetables. Set broth aside and keep warm.

Preheat the oven to 350°F (180°C, gas mark 4).

Break the head of cabbage down to its leaves. Bring a large saucepan of water to a boil and add the reserved vegetables. Add the cabbage leaves and boil until *al dente*. Remove cabbage, drain, and cut into thin strips. Arrange on a large clean dishtowel to dry. Strain cooking liquid, discard vegetables and reserve cooking liquid for another use.

Generously butter a 13-cup (3¼-liter) capacity, deep casserole dish. Arrange one-third of the bread slices on the bottom, cover with one-third of the sliced cabbage, and then one-third of the cheese. Repeat layers ending with a layer of cheese. Pour in 2½ cups (625 ml) of the warm broth and sprinkle the top with cinnamon.

Bake for 20 minutes or until lightly browned on top and firm. Remove from the oven and serve immediately. Serves 4 to 6.

ZUPPA DI CRESCIONE CON RANE

Watercress Soup with Frog Legs (Osteria di via Solata)

The once common sight in Lombardy of men fishing for frogs in the small canals that border the rice paddies is fast disappearing but frogs do remain an important and delicious menu item. ☺☺

6 cups (1¹/₂ liters) lightly salted water
1 small carrot, roughly chopped
1 small yellow or brown onion, quartered
1 rib celery with leaves, roughly chopped
1 medium rennet apple, peeled, cored, thinly sliced
2 small potatoes, peeled and cubed
3¹/₂ cups (420 g) tightly packed watercress leaves and stems, washed and thick stems removed
Salt to taste
Freshly ground black pepper to taste
4 tablespoons butter
8 frog legs, cleaned
¹/₄ cup (60 ml) dry white wine
1 tablespoon finely chopped fresh thyme
8 slices bread

In a large pot, bring the salted water to a boil. Add the carrot, onion, and celery and reduce heat to low. Simmer for 20 minutes. Strain, reserving broth and keeping vegetables for another use.

Return broth to the pot and bring to a boil. Add the apple slices, potato, and watercress and cook over medium heat until the apple and potato are tender, about 5 minutes.

Remove from heat and strain, reserving broth. Purée solids in a blender, adding enough of the broth to make a medium-thick purée. If not enough broth, add some water. Season to taste with salt and pepper. Set aside and keep warm.

Meanwhile, heat a skillet over medium heat. Melt the butter and add the frog legs. Cook for 2 minutes on each side or until lightly browned. Add the wine and thyme and season to taste with salt and pepper. Continue to cook until all the wine has been absorbed, about 5 minutes.

Toast the bread. Divide the warm watercress purée between 4 soup plates and arrange frog legs in the center of each plate. Serve immediately with slices of toasted bread. Serves 4 to 6.

"CASONSEI" ALLA BERGAMASCA

Bergamo-style Stuffed Pasta (Osteria di via Solata)

Casonsei are a horseshoe-shaped stuffed pasta. The simple sage and butter sauce is particularly tasty with the rich filling. ☺☺☺

> 1 portion pasta sheets (page 36)
> 9 tablespoons butter
> 3½ oz (100 g) ground veal
> 3½ oz (100 g) ground pork
> 3½ oz (100 g) ground beef
> 3½ oz (100 g) salami, any outer skin removed, finely chopped
> 6½ oz (200 g) *pancetta*, half diced, half julienned (keep separately)
> ½ teaspoon salt, or to taste
> ¼ teaspoon freshly ground black pepper, or to taste
> 1 teaspoon finely chopped fresh parsley
> 6 tablespoons grated Grana cheese
> 2 eggs
> 2 tablespoons finely shredded fresh sage leaves

Prepare the pasta sheets, following the instructions of page 36. Cut pasta into sixteen 1⅔ x 3¼-in (4 x 8-cm) rectangles of pasta.

To make the stuffing, melt 2 tablespoons of the butter in a medium skillet over high heat. Add the veal, pork, beef, salami, and diced pancetta. Cook until browned, about 10 minutes, stirring occasionally. Remove from heat and cool. Add salt and pepper, parsley, 1 tablespoon of the grated Grana cheese, and the eggs. Stir well.

Divide stuffing into 16 and place in the center of each rectangle. Fold rectangles in half and seal tightly by pressing around the borders. Bend each rectangle into a horseshoe shape. Place pasta on a clean, floured dishtowel, making sure the sides are not touching. Cover with another clean, floured dishtowel and set aside.

To cook the pasta, bring a large saucepan of generously salted water to a boil. Add the *casonsei* and stir them gently. When cooked *al dente*, about 3 minutes after the water returns to a boil, remove with a slotted spoon and divide between 4 individual pasta plates.

While the pasta is cooking, melt the remaining butter in a small saucepan until foaming. Julienne remaining *pancetta* and add to butter along with the sage. Sauté until nicely browned. Sprinkle with remaining cheese, then top pasta with the *pancetta* and sage-melted butter. Serve immediately with additional grated cheese, if desired.

RAVIOLI DI RANE

Frog Leg Ravioli (Ristorante Il Griso)

Local shrimp and frogs feature prominently in many Lombardy dishes. ☻☻☻

1 portion pasta dough (page 36)
1 portion watercress purée (page 37)
1 tablespoon all-purpose (plain) flour
Salt to taste
Freshly ground white pepper to taste
10 frog legs, boned
7 tablespoons butter
2 cloves garlic, finely chopped
3 shallots, finely chopped
$^3/_4$ cup (180 ml) dry white wine
$^3/_4$ cup (180 ml) vegetable broth
$^1/_2$ cup (125 ml) cream
1 large tomato, skinned, seeded, diced
6 sprigs chervil

Prepare the two sheets of pasta (page 36) and set aside. Prepare watercress purée (page 37); set aside.

To make the filling, season flour with salt and pepper and add frog legs. Toss until lightly coated. Melt 2 tablespoons of the butter in a skillet over medium heat, add half of the garlic and shallot and cook for 2 minutes or until shallot is transparent. Add the frog legs and cook for 3 minutes, stirring constantly. Remove from heat and set-aside. when cool, divide frog legs into 20 portions.

Bring the two thin sheets of prepared pasta to the work surface. On one sheet of dough, place the 20 pieces of frog leg mixture equidistant apart. Dip a finger in water and lightly wet the area between the filling. Place the second pasta sheet on top. Press dough to seal; cut into half-moon shaped ravioli.

Melt 1 tablespoon of the butter in a saucepan over medium heat. Add the remaining garlic and shallots and cook until transparent, about 2 minutes. Add the wine and cook until almost completely evaporated, about 3 minutes. Add the broth and cook for 5 minutes or until reduced by two-thirds, stirring occasionally. Add the cream and cook, stirring frequently, for about 2 minutes or until the sauce starts to thicken slightly and have a creamy consistency. Stir in the watercress purée and season to taste with salt and pepper. Remove from heat, cut the remaining 4 tablespoons butter into pieces and add gradually, stirring between additions.

Meanwhile, bring a large pot of salted water to a boil and add the ravioli. Stir carefully with a wooden spoon and cook until *al dente*. Drain gently and divide among 4 warm pasta plates. Place 1 tablespoon of diced tomato and a sprig of chervil in the center of each plate. Pour watercress cream over pasta and serve immediately.

AGNOLOTTI

Stuffed Pasta (Il Cambio)

🕐🕐🕐

1 portion pasta sheets (page 36)
¹/₄ cup (60 ml) extra-virgin olive oil
12 oz (400 g) veal shoulder
8 oz (250 g) pork thigh
1 small carrot, roughly chopped into
  1¹/₄-in (3-cm) pieces
1 medium onion, quartered
1 sprig rosemary
1 cup (250 ml) dry white wine
2 cups (500 ml) boiling beef broth
2 cups (175 g) spinach, washed roots removed
1 egg
¹/₃ cup (85 g) grated Grana cheese
Pinch ground nutmeg
¹/₄ teaspoon freshly ground white pepper,
  or to taste
¹/₄ teaspoon salt, or to taste
2 tablespoons butter, cut into pieces

Prepare the pasta sheets (page 36) and set aside. Preheat oven to 350°F (180°C, gas mark 4).

Heat oil in a large ovenproof pot or saucepan with a tight-fitting lid over medium heat. Brown the veal and pork on all sides. Add the carrot, onion, rosemary, and wine and cook for 5 to 6 minutes, basting occasionally, until the wine has evaporated. Add boiling broth to the meat, cover and cook in the oven for 45 minutes or until meat is extremely tender. Remove the meat from the pot and cool.

Discard rosemary and strain remaining cooking liquid and reserve. Cook spinach in a medium pan of lightly salted water for 2 to 3 minutes or until wilted and bright green. Drain, run under cold water, and squeeze gently to remove any excess liquid. When the meat has cooled completely, finely chop or place in a food processor and process until finely chopped, along with the spinach. Place spinach and meat mixture in a bowl. Add the egg, cheese, nutmeg, salt, and pepper. Mix thoroughly.

Bring the two thin sheets of prepared pasta to the work surface. On half of one of the sheets, place 12 even sized piles of stuffing about ¹/₂ in (1 cm) apart. Fold the dough over so that the empty side covers the balls of stuffing.

Using a 1-in (2¹/₂-cm) round cutter, cut the *agnolotti* and transfer to a clean, lightly floured dishtowel. Repeat with remaining sheet. Bring a large pot of generously salted water to a boil. Add the *agnolotti* and stir gently. When cooked *al dente*, about 3 minutes after the water returns to a boil, remove them with a slotted spoon to a serving platter.

Place reserved meat cooking liquid in a small saucepan and bring to the boil. Remove from heat and pour over cooked *agnolotti*. Top with butter and Grana cheese and serve immediately, passing additional grated cheese.

UOVA IN PASTA TARTUFATE

Truffled Egg Ravioli (Belvedere)

This mouthwatering dish of ravioli stuffed with spinach and two types of cheese is further enriched by the addition of grated white Alba truffle. ②②②

1 portion egg ravioli dough (page 36)
2 cups (175 g) spinach, washed and roots removed
6¹/₂ oz (200 g) ricotta
8 tablespooons grated Parmesan cheese
Pinch ground nutmeg
¹/₂ teaspoon salt, or to taste
¹/₄ teaspoon freshly ground white pepper, or to taste
10 eggs
10 tablespoons butter, cubed
1 white Alba truffle

Prepare the egg ravioli dough (page 36) and set aside.

Cook spinach in a medium saucepan of lightly salted water until wilted and bright green. Drain and squeeze gently to remove any excess liquid.

To make the filling, in a bowl combine the ricotta, spinach, 2 tablespoons of the Parmesan cheese, nutmeg, salt, and pepper. Add 2 of the eggs and mix well to combine.

Flour work surface lightly and return dough to lightly floured work surface. Cut dough into two pieces, and keep one covered while working with the other. Use your hands to flatten the ball slightly, then roll out the dough with a lightly floured rolling pin, turning it a quarter turn in between each roll. When the dough is ¹/₈ in thick, complete a final thinning of the pasta by wrapping about one-third of it around the rolling pin and rapidly rolling back and forth. Repeat with remaining dough, making two sheets of pasta dough that are very thin and as similar to each other in size and shape as possible.

Place spinach filling in a pastry tube. Lay one of the sheets of dough on the work surface. Pipe the filling in 8 spots, equidistant apart, leaving an indentation in the center of each portion of filling.

Carefully separate the remaining 8 eggs, keeping the yolks separate from each other. Very gently place 1 yolk in each filling indentation, taking care to leave the yolks whole. Carefully place the second sheet of dough over the filling and cut with a 2-in (5-cm) round cutter. Seal edges firmly.

Place pasta on a floured tray. Melt butter in a small saucepan, set aside and keep warm. Bring a large pot of salted water to boil and gently add the pasta. Cook 2 minutes. Remove with a slotted spoon or skimmer and divide among 4 warm soup plates. Sprinkle on remaining Parmesan cheese, pour on the melted butter, and shave on a generous amount of Alba truffle. Serve immediately.

TAGLIOLINI AL BURRO E TARTUFO

Tagliolini with Butter and Truffle (La Contea)

Tagliolini are thin egg noodles that are also known as *taglierini, tagliatini,* and, in the Piedmont dialect, *tajarin*. This elegant dish highlights the luxurious flavor of truffle. ☻

> ***Tagliolini* (or other thin) pasta, fresh or dried**
> **1 cup (250 ml) beef broth**
> **8 tablespoons butter, cubed**
> **7 tablespoons grated Grana cheese**
> **Salt to taste**
> **Freshly ground white pepper**
> **1 white truffle, lightly scrubbed, thinly sliced**

To prepare the sauce, place beef broth, butter, and cheese in a small saucepan over medium heat. Stir constantly with a wooden spoon until cheese melts and forms a sauce, taking care not to let the mixture start to simmer or boil. Season to taste with salt and pepper.

Bring a large pot of salted water to a boil. Toss in the pasta, separating and stirring them with a long-handled fork. Cook for 3 to 4 minutes or until just *al dente* (fresh *tagliolini* cook very quickly; start tasting as soon as the noodles rise to the surface of the water). For dried pasta, follow the instructions on the packet.

Drain *tagliolini* and place in a warm serving bowl. Pour sauce and top and toss gently. Sprinkle thin slices of white truffle on top. Serve immediately, passing additional grated cheese on the side, if desired. Serves 4 to 6.

PIZZOCCHERI

Buckwheat Pasta (Osteria di via Solata)

Pizzoccheri are a hearty buckwheat pasta. They are almost always prepared with cheese and cabbage. The result is a perfect winter dish. 🕐🕐🕐

1 portion buckwheat pasta dough (page 35)
3 medium potatoes, peeled and cubed
$^1/_2$ small head Savoy cabbage, about 1$^2/_3$ lb (800 g), thinly sliced
4 tablespoons butter
3 cloves garlic, cut in halves
2 fresh sage leaves, shredded
3 cups (375 g) Lean Valtellina cheese such as Scemut

Prepare the buckwheat pasta dough (page 35) and set aside.

Bring a large pot of salted water to a boil. Add the potatoes and cabbage and cook for 3 to 4 minutes or until potatoes are almost cooked through. Add the pasta, stir well to combine and cook for a further 3 minutes or until pasta is cooked but still *al dente*.

Meanwhile, melt the butter in a small saucepan over medium heat. Add the garlic and sage and cook for 1 to 2 minutes or until garlic is golden. Discard garlic.

Drain cooked pasta, potatoes, and cabbage. Spread one-third of the mixture in a thin layer in a medium serving dish. Sprinkle on one-third of the cheese. Repeat with remaining mixture and cheese. Top with the melted butter. Serve immediately.

Serves 4 to 6.

GNOCCHI ALLA CONTADINA

Country-style Gnocchi (La Contea)

This recipe offers one simple serving suggestion for gnocchi, but they marry well with all kinds of sauces. In addition to serving them with butter and cheese, try them with a fresh tomato sauce, possibly one that incorporates vegetables and herbs. ◑◑

2 lb (1 kg) starchy potatoes, boiled or steamed until tender, cooled and peeled
Salt to taste
2 tablespoons butter, cubed
2 cups (250 g) all-purpose (plain) flour, sifted
2 egg yolks
Pinch nutmeg
4 tablespoons grated Grana cheese, or to taste
8 tablespoons butter, melted

Mash well or push peeled, cooked potatoes through a ricer, letting the results fall into a medium bowl. Using a wooden spoon, stir in the butter, egg yolks, nutmeg and enough flour to form a soft dough. You may not use all of the flour. (If you are unsure of the correct consistency for gnocchi dough, bring a small pot of water to a boil, pinch off a piece of dough, and boil it. It should rise to the surface soon after you add it to the water, and it should not taste excessively heavy.) Let cool.

Divide the dough into 3 or 4 pieces and between floured hands, roll each piece into a long sausage, about $^3/_4$ in ($1^1/_2$ cm) wide. Cut into pieces about $^1/_2$ in (2 cm) long. Press the side of each dumpling against a fork, pressing lightly with your thumb, to curve the gnocchi and make grooves on one side.

Arrange the gnocchi on a lightly floured clean dishtowel, cover with another lightly floured clean dishtowel, and set them aside to rest for 1 to 2 hours.

When you are ready to cook the gnocchi, bring a large pot of salted water to a boil. Add the gnocchi and stir gently. As the gnocchi rise to the surface, remove them with a slotted spoon and transfer to a warm serving dish. Sprinkle on the cheese and pour on the melted butter. Mix gently and serve immediately. Serves 6.

RISOTTO ALLA MILANESE

Milanese Risotto (Antica Osteria del Ponte)

There are as many versions of this famous Milanese dish as there are inhabitants of Milan, maybe more. This is ours. Some versions call for adding the wine before the rice, or using red wine, or substituting shallots for the onion, and so on. ◐ ◑

5 cups (1¼ liters) beef or chicken broth
Pinch saffron strands
Pinch saffron powder
10 tablespoons butter, cubed
1 oz (30 g) marrow
1 small onion, finely chopped
¼ teaspoon freshly ground black pepper, or
to taste
2 cups (440 g) Carnaroli rice
1 cup (250 ml) dry white wine
6 tablespoons grated Grana cheese, or to taste
Extra grated Grana cheese, for serving on the
side

Place broth in a medium saucepan over high heat and bring to a boil. Reduce heat to very low and keep warm until needed. Place saffron pistils and powder in a small cup. Add 1 tablespoon of hot broth. Stir to combine and set aside.

Heat a large saucepan over medium heat and melt 2 tablespoons of the butter. Add the bone marrow, and onion and cook for 5 minutes, stirring occasionally, or until onion is transparent.

Increase heat to high, add the rice and cook for 1 minute or until the reice grains are transparent, stirring constantly. Add the wine and cook until it is absorbed, about 2 minutes. Add 2 cups (500 ml) of the warm broth and the reserved saffron broth and continue to cook, stirring constantly. As the broth is absorbed, add a little more, about ½ cup (125 ml). Continue to cook this way, adding small amounts of hot broth, until the rice is cooked *al dente*.

Move the saucepan off the heat. Allow the risotto to rest for 1 minute. Cut remaining butter into pieces and stir through risotto with the grated cheese until combined and rice is creamy. Divide between 4 pasta bowls and serve immediately. Pass additional grated cheese on the side. Serves 4 to 6.

RISOTTINO AL BAROLO

Rice with Barolo (Il Cambio)

This simple but rich rice dish takes on an appealing maroon color from the addition of red Barolo wine. ✆✆

4 cups (1 liter) beef broth
2 cups (500 ml) Barolo or any dry, red wine
1 tablespoon extra-virgin olive oil
1 small onion, finely chopped
2 cups (440 g) Semifino Vialone Nano rice
¹/₂ teaspoon salt, or to taste
8 tablespoons butter, cubed
4 tablespoons grated Grana cheese
Extra grated Grana cheese for serving

Place broth in a medium saucepan over high heat and bring to a boil. Heat the wine in a small saucepan over high heat and bring to a boil. Reduce heat to very low and keep warm until needed.

Heat a large saucepan over medium heat. Add the oil and heat. Add onion and cook for 5 minutes or until translucent. Add the rice and salt, and cook for 1 minute or until rice grains are transparent, stirring constantly.

Add the warmed wine and cook without stirring until the rice has absorbed all of the wine. Add 2 cups (500 ml) of the warmed broth and continue to cook, stirring constantly. As the broth is absorbed, add a little more broth, about ¹/₂ cup (125 ml) at a time. Continue to cook this way, adding small amounts of hot broth, until the rice is cooked *al dente*. Adjust salt to taste.

Remove from heat and stir through butter and Grana cheese. Cover, and allow to rest for 1 minute.

Transfer risotto to a serving platter and serve immediately, passing additional grated cheese on the side. Serves 4 to 6.

FONDUTA ALLA VALDOSTANA

Cheese Fondue (Chez Pierre)

With so few ingredients, the quality of the cheese is really important here. Be sure to look for the best. ⏱

3 cups (750 g) Fontina Valdostana cheese
1¹⁄₂ cups (375 ml) milk
2 egg yolks
Bread or polenta squares
White truffle, optional

Cut the rind from the cheese and dice. In a large saucepan, combine the cheese and milk, cover with a tight-fitting lid, and let sit overnight in a cool place. Just before serving, place saucepan over very low heat and stir constantly with a wooden spoon for 10 to 15 minutes or until cheese has melted and the mixture is creamy. Add the egg yolks one at a time stirring to combine them. The mixture should remain smooth and creamy.

Pour the fondue into 4 individual warm serving dishes or a medium, warm fondue pot, and serve immediately accompanied by bread or polenta. If using white truffle, shave liberally over the top of each dish. Serves 4 to 6.

FLAN DI CARDI E TOPINAMBOUR CON FONDUTA

Cardoon and Jerusalem Artichoke Flan with Cheese Sauce (La Contea)

🕙🕙🕙

1 portion cheese sauce (page 39)
8 oz (250 g) cardoons, peeled and cut into long slices (rub with lemon to prevent discoloration)
2 tablespoons extra-virgin olive oil
1 sprig rosemary
1 clove garlic, crushed
1 small carrot, finely chopped
1 small onion, finely chopped
1 rib celery, finely chopped
8 oz (250 g) Jerusalem artichokes, cubed
4 tablespoons butter, cubed
$^1/_3$ cup (40 g) all-purpose (plain) flour
4 eggs, separated
$^1/_2$ teaspoon salt, or to taste
$^1/_4$ teaspoon freshly ground white pepper, or to taste
1 tablespoon butter, extra
1 tablespoon all-purpose (plain) flour, extra
2 teaspoons grated Parmesan cheese
$^1/_2$ teaspoon ground nutmeg

Start preparing the cheese sauce the night before the meal (see page 39). The next day, preheat oven to 350°F (180°C, gas mark 4). Bring a large pot of lightly salted water to a boil and cook the cardoons until they are still quite crisp. Drain and, when cool enough to handle, cube. Set aside. In a large pan over medium heat, heat the oil. Add the rosemary, garlic, carrot, onion, and celery. Cook for 3 minutes or until golden.

Add the cardoons and artichokes and cook for 5 minutes or until still a little crunchy, stirring occasionally. Remove from heat. Discard rosemary and garlic.

To prepare the béchamel, in a small pot, heat the remaining milk without allowing it to boil. In a pan, melt the butter over medium heat. Add flour and cook, stirring, for 1 minute or until the mixture looks like wet sand. Gradually add the warm milk to the flour and butter mixture and stir to combine. Add nutmeg, salt, and pepper and continue cooking, stirring constantly, as the mixture slowly comes to a boil. Remove from the heat and strain the béchamel through a sieve.

Whip the egg whites until stiff. Fold the cardoons and artichokes into the béchamel, stir in the egg yolks and the Parmesan cheese. Very gradually and carefully fold in the whipped egg whites to combine the ingredients while retaining as much volume as possible. Season to taste with salt and pepper.

Grease and lightly flour a 13-cup (3$^1/_4$-liter) capacity casserole with the extra butter and flour and place in a deep baking dish with enough water to reach one-third up the sides of the casserole dish. Cook in the oven for about 45 minutes or until firm. Meanwhile, finish preparing the cheese sauce. Unmold the flan onto a warm serving plate and pour the cheese sauce over it. Serves 4 to 6.

ANGUILLA IN CARPIONE

Vinegar-marinated Eel (La Contea)

This is an old recipe, dating back to the 1600s. People kept it on hand so that they would always have something to serve to guests. Eel is prevalent in the Tanaro river. After the eel is cooked, it is marinated for two days before serving. ⏱⏱

6 small eel fillets, about 10 oz (300 g), washed and cut into 1²/₃-in (4-cm) long pieces
3 tablespoons all-purpose (plain) flour
4 tablespoons extra-virgin olive oil

Marinade

3 tablespoons extra-virgin olive oil
¹/₂ large onion, finely sliced
3 cloves garlic, crushed
1 tablespoon finely chopped fresh sage
¹/₄ teaspoon salt
¹/₄ teaspoon freshly ground white pepper
¹/₂ cup (125 ml) strong white wine vinegar
1 cup (250 ml) dry white wine

To prepare the **marinade**, combine the olive oil, onion, garlic, sage, salt, and pepper in a small saucepan. Place over medium heat and cook for 3 minutes or until the onion just starts to turn golden; do not allow it to brown. Add the vinegar and wine and increase heat to high. Bring mixture to a boil, then remove from the heat and set aside to cool to room temperature.

Dredge eel pieces lightly in flour. Heat a medium frying pan over high heat and add the oil. Heat until it just begins to smoke. Add the eel pieces and cook for 2 minutes each side or until golden brown on all sides. Remove eel with a slotted spoon or skimmer and transfer to a bowl. Pour on the marinade and marinate eel in a cool place for 48 hours before serving. Serves 4 to 6.

FILETTO DI LAVARELLO DEL LAGO DI LECCO

Lake Lecco Whitefish (Ristorante Il Griso)

4 whole firm whitefish, about 12 oz (375 g) each
1 medium leek, thinly sliced lengthwise into
    matchsticks
1 sprig thyme
$\frac{1}{2}$ large onion, sliced
$\frac{1}{2}$ large carrot, roughly chopped
$\frac{1}{2}$ cup (125 ml) dry white wine
2 teaspoons salt, or to taste
8 cups (2 liters) water
6 tablespoons extra-virgin olive oil
1 clove garlic, halved
3 medium zucchini (courgette), cut lengthwise
    into matchsticks
2 medium carrots, cut lengthwise into matchsticks
6 baby onions, halved
1 tablespoon white sugar
4 tablespoons red wine vinegar
2 tablespoons butter, cut into pieces
$\frac{1}{4}$ teaspoon freshly ground white pepper, or
    to taste

To prepare fish, clean and fillet them, reserving the heads and bones. Then reconstruct the fillets into a fish shape, tying them with the leek strips.

To prepare fish fumet, place fish heads and bones in a large saucepan. Add thyme, onion, chopped carrot, wine, half of the salt, and water. Bring to a boil, then reduce heat and simmer for 30 minutes. Strain fumet and reserve.

Place the sugar into a medium saucepan over very low heat and cook, stirring, for 1 minutes or until melted and starting to turn a light brown colour. Add the vinegar and $\frac{1}{2}$ cup (125 ml) of the fish fumet. Increase heat to medium and bring to the boil. Cook for 5 minutes or until liquid is reduced by half. Set caramel sauce aside and keep warm. Meanwhile, heat 3 tablespoons of the olive oil in a skillet over medium heat with the garlic. Cook the zucchini, carrots, and baby onions individually until *al dente*, removing each with a slotted spoon to a medium bowl and keeping warm. When all the vegetables have been cooked, discard garlic clove halves. Return vegetables to skillet and pour the caramel sauce over them. Cook, stirring constantly, for two minutes or until just heated through. Remove from heat and keep vegetables warm.

Heat a large skillet over medium heat and add the butter with the remaining 3 tablespoons of oil. When butter is melted arrange the fish in a single layer. Season to taste with pepper and the remaining. Cook for 4 minutes each side or until fish flakes with a fork and is lightly browned on each side. If fish is starting to stick to bottom of skillet, add 1 tablespoon water to the pan. Place one fish in the center of 4 individual plates. Using a slotted spoon, divide vegetables evenly amongst the plates, placing in a neat pile next to the fish. Spoon any remaining caramel sauce over the fish and serve immediately.

PICCIONI ARROSTITI AL ROSMARINO

Roast Pigeons with Rosemary (Trattoria I Bologna)

This presentation for small fowl is a classic with the flavors of rosemary, garlic, and brandy guaranteed to please. ☻☻

6 tablespoons extra-virgin olive oil
4 young pigeons, cleaned, trimmed and halved
2 cloves garlic, crushed
9 sprigs rosemary
1 teaspoon salt
$^{1}/_{4}$ teaspoon freshly ground black pepper
1 tablespoon extra virgin olive oil, extra
$^{1}/_{2}$ cup (125 ml) brandy

Preheat the oven to 400°F (200°C, gas mark 6).

Heat a large skillet over high heat. Heat half of the oil, then add the pigeons and cook for 8 to 10 minutes or until browned on all sides.

Grease a large, deep casserole dish, about 3 liter (12 cup) capacity, with the remaining oil. Add the garlic and 3 sprigs rosemary, stirring to evenly distribute. Add browned pigeons and salt and pepper, tossing to coat. Drizzle with extra oil and place casserole in oven. Cook for 30 minutes, basting occasionally with the liquid that gathers at the bottom of the casserole.

When pigeons are almost cooked through, add brandy to casserole. Return to oven and cook for 5 minutes more or until brandy has evaporated.

Arrange the pigeons on 4 individual serving plates and spoon over cooking liquid. Garnish plates with remaining sprigs rosemary and serve immediately.

FAGIANELLA ALL' ARNEIS

Pheasant with Arneis Sauce (La Contea)

When it comes to pheasants, the female is less attractive but tastier. Pheasants should not be cooked immediately after slaughter, but should instead be hung and aged for some time. Consult a reliable butcher. ☻☻

1 aged whole pheasant, about 2 lb (1 kg),
    cleaned and cut into parts
$^1/_2$ teaspoon salt
$^1/_4$ teaspoon freshly ground black pepper
7 tablespoons extra-virgin olive oil
2 tablespoons lard
1 medium carrot, roughly cubed
2 ribs celery, roughly cubed
3 cloves garlic, thinly sliced
6 juniper berries, crushed
$^1/_2$ cup (125 ml) dry Marsala
$^1/_2$ cup (125 ml) Arneis or dry white wine
$^1/_2$ cup (125 ml) beef broth
2 tablespoons tomato purée
3 tablespoons finely chopped fresh parsley

Season the pheasant parts with salt and pepper to taste. Heat a medium pan over medium heat. Add 4 tablespoons of the oil and heat. Add the pheasant parts and cook for 4 to 5 minutes or until browned on all sides. Remove from pan and set aside.

Heat a large pan over medium heat. Add the remaining 3 tablespoons of oil and lard and heat. Add carrot, celery, garlic, and juniper berries and cook, stirring occasionally, for 3 to 4 minutes or until golden brown. Add the browned pheasant parts, Marsala and Arneis and cook for 8 to 10 minutes or until liquid has evaporated.

Add beef stock and cook for a further 3 minutes or until pheasant is cooked through and tender, stirring occasionally,. Add the tomato purée and parsley and cook a further 2 to 3 minutes or until well combined.

Remove pheasant pieces with a slotted spoon and arrange on a warm serving platter. Strain the cooking liquid through a very fine sieve or place in a food processor and process until smooth. Spoon sauce over the pheasant and serve immediately.

"POLENTA E OSEI" ALLA BERGAMASCA

Bergamo-style Polenta and Game Birds (Osteria di via Solata)

Traditionally, polenta is prepared in a large copper pot known as a *paiolo*, but it will be just as tasty cooked in other types of cookware. Although the cooking time here may seem excessive, don't try and skimp on it. You will end up with undercooked polenta that is bitter and hard to digest. ②②

8 cups (2 liters) water
1¹/₂ tablespoons rock salt
2¹/₂ cups (425 g) coarse-ground cornmeal
4 tablespoons butter, cubed, extra
4 small game birds, cleaned, trimmed and trussed
2 teaspoons salt
¹/₄ teaspoon freshly ground black pepper
5¹/₂ tablespoons butter
4 fresh bay leaves
¹/₂ cup (125 ml) dry white wine

To make the polenta, in a large saucepan, bring the water and rock salt to a boil. As soon as it begins to boil, add cornmeal very slowly and gradually in a thin stream, stirring constantly with a wooden spoon. Continue stirring constantly and in the same direction until the polenta is extremely thick (stirring should be difficult) and can be pulled away from the sides of the pan, approximately 25 to 30 minutes. Remove from heat and stir through extra butter. Cover, set aside and keep warm.

Meanwhile, season the birds with salt and pepper. Heat a large heatproof terracotta casserole dish or heavy based skillet over medium heat. Add butter and when melted add bay leaves and birds. Cook for 10 to 12 minutes or until they are golden brown on all sides. Increase heat to high and add the white wine. Cook for 5 to 8 minutes or until almost all the wine has evaporated, turning occasionally. Reduce heat to low and cook for 8 to 10 minutes or until birds are cooked through and tender, turing occasionally. Add a small amount of warm water if birds are not cooked enough and are sticking to the bottom of the pan.

Remove birds from heat and serve in the casserole dish or heated serving dish. Pour warm polenta onto a large wooden board and bring the board to the table. Serve immediately.

"FOIJOEU"

Tripe (Osteria di via Solata)

The tripe for this recipe should be mostly the smooth kind with a small amount of honeycomb tripe as well. Even when cooked, the tripe will have a dense texture. ② ②

$^1/_2$ cup (125 g) large white beans, soaked overnight and drained
1$^1/_2$ cups (375 ml) beef broth
1 medium onion, cut into $^2/_3$-in (1$^1/_2$-cm) cubes
6 tablespoons butter, cubed
2 lb (1 kg) tripe, cleaned and prepared for cooking, cut into $^1/_4$-in ($^1/_2$-cm) strips
2 tablespoons fat from roast meat
3 tablespoons tomato purée
1 medium carrot, thinly sliced
1 rib celery, thinly sliced
$^1/_2$ teaspoon salt
$^1/_4$ teaspoon freshly ground black pepper
3 tablespoons grated Grana cheese
Grated Grana cheese for serving, extra

Cook beans in lightly salted water until soft, then drain. Set aside. Place beef broth in a small saucepan and bring to a boil. Reduce heat to very low, cover and keep warm.

Heat a heatproof terracotta pot or large saucepan over medium heat. Add the butter and when melted add the onion. Cook for 2 to 3 minutes or until onion is transparent. Add the tripe and cook for 2 minutes. Add the roast meat fat, tomato puree, carrot and celery and cook a further 2 to 3 minutes.

Add 1 cup (125 ml) of the warm broth or enough to almost cover tripe, and bring to a boil. Cover, reduce heat to low and Add salt and pepper and the cooked beans. Increase heat to medium and cook for a further 3 to 4 minutes or until ingredients are well combined. Serve on a heated platter, sprinkled with grated cheese and serve immediately, with a side dish of extra cheese on the side. Serves 4 to 6.

OSSIBUCHO

Ossibucho (Osteria di via Solata)

Slow-cooked veal shanks become unbelievably tender. Traditionally, this dish is served alongside Risotto alla Milanese (page 68), but it is also delicious served with plain white rice. ◑ ◑

8 small veal shanks
$^1/_4$ cup (30 g) all-purpose (plain) flour
8 tablespoons butter
$^1/_2$ teaspoon salt or to taste
$^1/_4$ teaspoon freshly ground black pepper
2 teaspoons grated lemon zest
1 teaspoon dried marjoram, crumbled
1 medium yellow or brown onion, finely
  chopped
1 medium carrot, finely chopped
1 rib celery, finely chopped
2 cloves garlic, finely chopped
1 cup (250 ml) dry white wine
2 tablespoons tomato purée
3 cups (750 ml) beef broth

Lightly dredge the veal shanks in flour. Place a large saucepan over medium heat. Add 6 tablespoons of the butter and, when melted, add the veal shanks. Sprinkle with the salt and pepper and cook the shanks for 6 to 8 minutes or until they are browned on both sides. Add lemon zest, marjoram, onion, carrot, celery, and half of the garlic. Cook for a further 4 minutes or until onion is transparent. Add the wine and cook for 6 to 8 minutes or until almost all of it has evaporated. Add tomato purée and 2 cups (500 ml) of the beef broth.

Cover the pan, reduce heat to low and simmer for 1 hour or until shanks are well cooked through and very tender, stirring and turning the shanks occasionally. If necessary, add more broth if the sauce is getting too thick.

Just before the veal shanks are done, add the remaining garlic. When veal shanks are cooked, add the remaining 2 tablespoons of butter in small pieces, allowing each piece to be incorporated before adding another. When all the butter has been added, cook for a further 2 minutes.

Remove veal shanks with a slotted spoon and arrange them on a platter. Pour sauce over veal shanks and serve immediately.

BRASATO AL BAROLO

Barolo-braised Beef (Osteria di via Solata)

This is the Northern Italian version of pot roast, with meat that practically melts in your mouth and the bracing flavor of local Barolo wine. ⏱⏱

2 lb (1 kg) rump roast, trimmed and tied with kitchen twine
2 medium carrots, roughly cubed
1 large onion, unpeeled and cut into 8 equal pieces
1 bouquet garni of 1 sprig parsley, 1 sprig thyme, 1 bay leaf, and 2 cloves
2 cloves garlic, halved
4 black peppercorns
1 teaspoon salt
1 bottle (750 ml) Barolo or any dry, red wine
3 tablespoons butter, cubed
$\frac{1}{4}$ cup (60 ml) brandy
$\frac{1}{2}$tablespoons tomato paste

Place the meat in a large bowl. Add the carrots, onions, bouquet garni, garlic, peppercorns and salt. Add wine and marinate for at least 8 hours but no more than 24 hours, turning occasionally. Drain meat reserving marinade and vegetables. Remove garlic and peppercorns from marinade and discard. Dry meat carefully by blotting with kitchen paper.

Heat a large pot over medium heat, add butter and, when melted, add meat and brown on all sides. Add the brandy and cook for 1 minutes to heat.

Carefully light the surface of the brandy and for 2 minutes or until the brandy is no longer flaming. Add the tomato paste, reserved marinade, vegetables and bouquet garni and bring to a boil. Reduce heat to low, cover and cook for $2\frac{1}{2}$ hours or until meat is cooked through and tender, turning occasionally.

Drain meat and vegetables, reserving cooking liquid and vegetables, and place meat on a large plate covered with aluminum foil. Stand in a warm place for 5 minutes to allow the meat juices to settle. Remove twine, slice meat and arrange it in a fan shape on a warm serving plate.

Remove bouquet garni from reserved vegetables and discard. Using a food processor or blender, process reserved vegetables and $1\frac{1}{2}$ cups (375 ml) of the reserved cooking liquid until smooth and a pourable, sauce consistency. Add more water if there is not enough cooking liquid. Spoon the sauce over the meat and serve immediately.

Serves 4 to 6.

COSTOLETTE DI VITELLO ALLA MILANESE

Milanese Veal Cutlets (Antica Osteria del Ponte)

This is one of Milan's most famous dishes, and as simple as it might sound, it is fabulous. If you wish, you may also season the cutlets with a small amount of grated nutmeg. ☉

4 veal cutlets, boned, lightly pounded to
  approximately $^1/_3$ **in (** $^3/_4$ **cm) thick**
Salt to taste
Freshly ground white pepper
$^1/_3$ **cup (40 g) all-purpose (plain) flour**
1 egg, lightly beaten
$^3/_4$ **cup (30 g) breadcrumbs**
$^1/_2$ **cup (100 g) butter**

Season cutlets to taste with salt and pepper. Dredge lightly in flour, then dip the cutlets in the beaten egg and then in the breadcrumbs. Press down lightly on the cutlets with the palms of your hands to attach the breadcrumbs.

Melt butter in a large skillet. When it is foaming, add the cutlets. Cook over medium heat until they are browned on both sides and tender, about 5 minutes per side. Remove cutlets with a slotted spatula and place on a warm serving dish. Pour the cooking butter over the cutlets. Salt lightly, if desired, and serve immediately.

STRACOTTO DI MANZO ALLE VERDURE

Beef and Vegetable Stew (Antica Osteria del Ponte)

For a more elegant presentation, after discarding the garlic and the bouquet garni, purée the remaining vegetables into a sauce. Traditionally, this is made in a *brasiera*, an oval or rectangular pan with a box-shaped lid. When the dish was cooked over a fire, the embers were spread over the top of the lid as well as underneath, so that the dish cooked in a perfectly uniform manner. 🕐🕐

3 lb (1^1/$_2$ kg) beef shank
1 teaspoon salt, or to taste
^{1}/$_2$ teaspoon freshly ground black pepper, or
   to taste
3^1/$_2$ tablespoons butter
2 tablespoons extra-virgin olive oil
6 tomatoes, cubed
1 large onion, halved and sliced
2 large carrots, thinly sliced
6 new potatoes, peeled and quartered
2 ribs celery, cut into ^{1}/$_2$-in (1-cm) slices
3 cloves garlic, unpeeled
1 bouquet garni of 1 sprig rosemary, 2 sage
   leaves, 1 sprig thyme, and 1 bay leaf
1 cup (250 ml) dry Marsala
1 cup (250 ml) water

Preheat oven to 400˚F (200˚C, gas mark 6).

Tie meat with kitchen twine and season with the salt and pepper.

Heat the butter and oil in a large, heavy-based saucepan. Add the tomatoes, onions, carrots, potatoes, celery, garlic, and bouquet garni and cook over medium heat for 6 to 8 minutes or until vegetables are softened, stirring occasionally,.

Place meat on top of the vegetables and add the Marsala and water. Cover the saucepan with a tight-fitting lid and place a heavy object on top to be sure it is closed securely. Place in the oven and roast for 2 hours or until tender and cooked through.

Remove from oven and transfer meat to a chopping board or tray. Cut away twine, slice meat into thin slices and arrange slices in a fan shape on a warm serving dish. Discard garlic and bouquet garni from vegetables and season to taste with remaining salt and pepper. Using a slotted spoon, garnish beef with cooked vegetables and moisten with any remaining cooking liquid. Serve immediately.

Serves 4 to 6.

"CARBONADE"

Braised Beef (Chez Pierre)

This famous dish has many variations. Curiously, a similar beef dish is made in Belgium using beer in place of the wine. At one time, true salt-cured beef was used, but today the beef is macerated in salt for several hours to approximate the taste. ☽ ☽

1¼ lb (600 g) beef filet
2 cloves garlic, minced
1 fresh bay leaf, minced
2 cloves, coarsely ground
1 tablespoon minced rosemary
2 teaspoons salt
⅓ cup (40 g) all-purpose (plain) flour
5 tablespoons butter
1 medium yellow or brown onion, thinly sliced
Freshly ground black pepper
2 cups (500 ml) red wine
Polenta, warm, or boiled new potatoes cooked
   with skins

Cut beef fillet into 4 even pieces and toss with the minced garlic, bay leaf, cloves, and rosemary until lightly coated. Place fillets in a small bowl, sprinkle with salt, and allow to macerate in the refrigerator for 4 hours or overnight.

Remove the fillet and brush off the herbs and the salt. Cut meat into strips and dredge in flour. Melt butter in a skillet and add the onion slices. Cook for 3 to 4 minutes or until golden brown. Add the beef, stir and cook until browned on all sides, about 7 minutes. Season to taste with salt and pepper and pour in the wine. Turn heat to low and continue cooking, stirring occasionally, for 8 to 10 minutes or until sauce has thickened.

Turn the *carbonade* onto a warm serving dish and serve immediately, with polenta (or potatoes) on the side.

LEPRE AL CIVET

Rabbit Stew (Belvedere)

This recipe takes a long time—the rabbit needs to cook for at least 3 hours—but not a lot of attention. ☉☉

1 medium rabbit, abut 2 lb (1 kg), cleaned
   and trimmed
2 cups (500 ml) beef broth
1 tablespoon lard
3 tablespoons butter
1 teaspoon salt
Polenta, warm

Marinade

6 cups (1$^1/_2$ liters) dry, red wine
1 medium carrot, roughly cubed
$^1/_2$ large yellow or brown onion, halved
1 rib celery
1 clove garlic, crushed
1 fresh bay leaf
1 cinnamon stick
3 cloves
3 black peppercorns
1 teaspoon salt

Cut rabbit in half lengthwise, then cut into 6 parts. Wash all parts thoroughly.

To prepare the **marinade**, combine red wine, carrot, onion, celery, garlic, bay leaf, cinnamon, cloves, peppercorns, and salt in a medium baking dish. Stir to combine, then add rabbit and marinate at least 12 hours, turning occasionally.

Place beef broth in a medium saucepan, bring to a boil, then reduce heat to very low and keep warm until needed.

Remove rabbit from marinade and dry carefully. Strain marinade reserving liquid and vegetables.

Heat a large, preferably copper pot over medium heat, add the lard and butter and stir until melted. Add the rabbit, salt, and marinated vegetables and spices and cook for 8 to 10 minutes or until rabbit is browned on all sides. Drain any excess fat from the pan and add enough of the warmed beef broth to just cover rabbit. Reduce heat to low, cover and simmer 1 hour, turning the rabbit occasionally and adding additional broth if the mixture is becoming dry. Add the reserved marinade liquid and continue cooking over low heat 1 hour and 40 minutes or until rabbit is very tender, turning the rabbit occasionally.

Remove bay leaf and cinnamon and discard. Remove rabbit from pot with a slotted spoon and keep warm. Place the vegetables in a food processor or blender with enough cooking liquid to make a slightly thick sauce. Arrange rabbit on a warm serving platter and pour sauce over top. Serve polenta on the side. Serves 4 to 6.

FILETTO DI CAVALLO ALLA PIASTRA

Horse Steak (Trattoria I Bologna)

A *piastra* is a slab of rock or a tile that is heated until very hot, then used either to cook food or simply to serve it so that it is sizzling as it reaches the table. Horse is best eaten medium rare and should be cooked quickly over high heat to prevent it from drying out and becoming tough. ✆

$\frac{1}{4}$ **cup finely chopped fresh marjoram, sage, oregano, thyme, and rosemary**
$\frac{1}{4}$ **cup finely chopped fresh parsley**
$\frac{1}{2}$ **cup (125 ml) extra-virgin olive oil**
2 tablespoons extra-virgin olive oil, extra
4 medium horse fillets, trimmed
1 large tomato, cubed
Salt and freshly ground white pepper to taste

Heat a *piastra* in the oven until very hot.

Combine herbs with the $\frac{1}{2}$ cup (125 ml) of oil and set aside.

Heat a large skillet over high heat until very hot. Place extra oil on a large plate and toss horse fillets in the oil until lightly coated. Transfer horse fillets to the hot pan, and cook for 4 minutes each side or until browned, turning once.

Arrange fillets on the preheated *piastra*. Pour on the herb sauce and sprinkle on the diced tomato. Season to taste with salt and pepper and serve immediately.

VITELLO TONNATO

Veal with Tuna Sauce (Trattoria I Bologna)

This is one of Italy's most famous dishes, and for good reason. In some versions, the veal is wrapped around anchovies, carrots, and drained pickles before being cooked in order to further flavor the meat. ⏱⏱

1½ lb (750 g) veal round, trussed
1 large carrot, sliced
1 large onion, sliced
2 ribs celery, sliced
1 cup (250 ml) dry white wine
1¾ cups (440 ml) extra-virgin olive oil
Zest and juice of 1 lemon
1½ teaspoons salt, or to taste
7-oz (210-g) can tuna in oil, drained
3 canned anchovy filets in oil, about ⅓ oz (10 g) drained
3 egg yolks
Small salted capers, soaked and drained, for garnish
Cornichon pickles, drained, for garnish

Place veal in a large casserole with a tight-fitting lid. Add carrot, onion, and celery. Pour in white wine, ¼ cup (60 ml) of the olive oil, and 2 cups (500 ml) cold water. Add the lemon zest and half of the juice. Cover and poach over medium-low heat until cooked through, about 1 hour.

Remove veal from casserole. Place a small wooden board on top of the veal and weigh it down. Set aside to cool.

Meanwhile, strain the cooking liquid, salt lightly, and return to heat. Bring cooking liquid to simmer and reduce to 3 tablespoons.

With a mortar and pestle or in a food processor, mash the tuna and anchovies to form a paste. Add the reduced cooking liquid and stir to combine.

To make the mayonnaise, place the egg yolks in a bowl with a pinch of salt and a few drops of the remaining lemon juice. Beat with a whisk while gradually adding remaining oil in a thin stream. After you have incorporated 4 or 5 tablespoons of oil, the sauce will begin to thicken. Add a few more drops of lemon juice and then continue to add oil (you may not need all of it). If the sauce seems too thick, simply add a few more drops of lemon juice.

Gradually add the tuna and anchovy mixture to the mayonnaise. Taste and adjust for salt.

Untie the veal and cut into thin slices.

Arrange the slices on a serving platter and pour sauce over veal. Garnish with capers and pickles. Serves 4 to 6.

FINANZIERA

Mixed Organ Meats (Il Cambio)

This is another of Piedmont's amazing arrays of meats, utilizing many of the more unusual types of offal. ②②②

   1 portion fried semolina squares (page 38)
   8 oz (250 g) calf's testicles, optional
   8 oz (250 g) veal sweetbreads
   4 oz (125 g) calf's brains
   3 oz (90 g) veal bone marrow
   3$\frac{1}{2}$ oz (100 g) chicken giblets
   5 tablespoons butter, cut in pieces
   5 shallots finely chopped
   2 bay leaves
   4 oz (120 g) *porcini* mushrooms in oil,
      drained and cubed
   $\frac{3}{4}$ cup (180 ml) dry Marsala
   4 oz (125 g) calf's liver, sliced
   1 small chicken breast, about 5 oz (150 g),
      cut into $\frac{1}{2}$-in (1-cm) thick slices
   3 tablespoons apple cider vinegar
   1 tablespoon balsamic vinegar
   2 cups (500 ml) oil for deep-frying
   1 teaspoon salt, or to taste

Prepare the fried semolina squares (page 38) and set aside.

Bring a medium saucepan of water to the boil and cook the testicles, sweetbreads, brains, marrow, and giblets separately for 3 to 4 minutes each or until almost cooked. Drain well, discard cooking liquid and set aside.

Heat a large saucepan over medium heat and add 2 tablespoons of the butter. When melted add the shallots and cook for 3 to 4 minutes or until golden. Add the cooked testicles, sweetbreads, marrow, giblets (but not the brains), the bay leaves, and mushrooms and cook for 5 minutes, stirring occasionally. Add the Marsala and cook for a further 5 minutes or until the Marsala is almost completely evaporated. Add the liver, chicken breast, apple cider and balsamic vinegars. Cook, stirring, for 1 minute, then add the brains and salt. Cook a further 2 minutes or until meats are cooked through, stirring continuously.

Remove and discard bay leaves from meat and add the remaining 3 tablespoons of the butter, scattering the pieces over the meat. Arrange the meat on a serving platter with the semolina squares and serve immediately. Serves 4 to 6.

"PAN DE MEIN"

Cornmeal Buns (Osteria di via Solata)

Traditionally, these sweet little buns are eaten on April 24, Saint George's Day. ✪ ✪

1¹/₂ cups (255 g) finely ground cornmeal
³/₄ cup (145 g) coarsely ground cornmeal
1¹/₂ cups (190 g) all-purpose (plain) flour
1 tablespoon dried yeast
¹/₄ cup (60 ml) milk, room temperature
3 eggs
10 tablespoons very soft butter
¹/₂ cup (80 g) confectioners' (icing) sugar
2 teaspoons elderberry flowers, optional
1 pinch salt
2 tablespoons vanilla sugar

Sift together the two types of cornmeal and the all-purpose flour. Dissolve the yeast in the milk.

On a large wooden cutting board or pasta board, shape the flour mixture into a well. Crack the eggs in the center. Add the butter, the powdered sugar, 1 teaspoon of elderberry flowers, the dissolved yeast and milk, and a pinch of salt to the well. Beat lightly with a finger. Draw in a small amount of flour from the side of the well and mix with the liquid until you have a paste. Add additional milk if necessary. Move the remaining flour from the well on top of the dough and knead to incorporate.

Shape the dough into a ball and place in a lightly floured bowl. Cover with a lightly floured clean dish-towel and let rise in a warm place for 1 hour or until doubled in size.

Line a baking sheet with aluminum foil and grease. Preheat oven to 350°F (180°C, gas mark 4).

Return the dough to the work surface. Divide into 8 even sized pieces. Shape each piece into a short round, about 4 in (10 cm) wide. Place on the baking sheet and sprinkle with remaining elderberry flowers and vanilla sugar.

Bake for 25 to 30 minutes or until lightly browned. Remove from oven and cool on baking sheet before carefully removing them.

Makes 8 buns.

CHARLOTTE DI MELE

Apple Charlotte (Antica Osteria del Ponte)

If you wish, you may warm up the rum before sprinkling it on, then flambé the charlotte once the rum has been added. If you can find it, use the bread known locally as *mistura*, which is made of white flour with a small amount of cornmeal, in place of the sandwich bread. ◑ ◑

- 1¹/₂ cups (375 g) white sugar
- 4 cups (1 liter) water
- 1 piece lemon peel
- ¹/₂ stick cinnamon
- 2 cloves
- 4 large rennet apples, peeled and cored
- 4 tablespoons butter, softened
- Ten ²/₃-in (1¹/₂-cm) thick slices of stale or fresh white sandwich bread
- ¹/₄ cup (60 g) white sugar, extra
- ¹/₂ cup (125 ml) apricot jam
- ¹/₂ cup (78 g) gold raisins, plumped in water, squeezed dry
- 2 tablespoons dark rum, or to taste

Preheat oven to 400˚F (200˚C, gas mark 6). Combine sugar, water, lemon peel, cinnamon, and cloves in a large saucepan. Place over high heat and bring to a boil.

Slice apples thinly, add to sugar syrup and place a small saucepan lid or plate on top to weight them down. Cook for 5 minutes or until *al dente*. Drain and set aside.

Butter the bread on one side , reserving some of the butter for coating the mold. Sprinkle with the extra sugar, reserving some for coating the mold. Cut bread into 1¹/₄-in (3-cm) wide pieces. Using the reserved butter, lightly grease a 13-cup (3¹/₄-liter) capacity charlotte mold, sprinkle with reserved extra sugar, and arrange the bread slices carefully around the sides and bottom of the mold, buttered side down, overlapping each piece and making sure there are no gaps or holes. Press lightly to seal. Fill the mold with one-third of the apple, one-third of the apricot jam, and one-third of the gold raisins. Repeat with remaining apples, jam and raisons, finishing with a layer of bread on top, buttered side down, carefully overlapping slices and ensuring there are no gaps or holes.

Bake charlotte in pre-heated oven for 35 minutes or until browned and firm. Remove from the oven and carefully unmold. Drizzle with rum and cut into wedges to serve. Serve immediately. Serves 8.

MELE RENETTE AL FORNO CON ZABAIONE

Baked Apples with Zabaione (Chez Pierre)

Zabaione can be a little temperamental. The trick is never to let the mixture come to a boil over the bain-marie. ☻☻

4 large rennet apples
4 amaretto cookies, crumbled
1 tablespoon gold raisins
1 tablespoon white sugar
7 tablespoons butter
Extra butter for greasing dish
$^1\!/_4$ cup (60 ml) water
4 egg yolks
$^1\!/_2$ cup (125 g) white sugar, extra
$^1\!/_3$ cup (85 ml) Muscat de Chambave or sweet
   white wine

Opposite right: Baked Apples with Zabaione; Opposite left: Baked Pears in Red Wine (see recipe on page 112)

Preheat oven to 400˚F (200˚C, gas mark 6).

Core apples reserving a small piece to plug the bottom of the apple to prevent the filling from falling out during cooking. In a small bowl, combine crumbled cookies, raisins, and sugar. Stuff apples with the raisin mixture and place a generous piece of butter on top of each apple. Lightly grease a medium baking dish with the extra butter and arrange apples on baking dish. Add water to dish, cover with aluminum foil and bake in preheated oven for about 40 minutes or until apples are soft and skin starts to split. Remove the apples from the oven and when still warm remove peel.

Meanwhile, fill a medium saucepan with enough water so that the base of a large bowl placed on top just touches the surface of the water. Place over high heat, bring to the boil, then reduce heat to medium.

To prepare the zabaione, place the egg yolks with the extra sugar into a large bowl and whisk until almost white. Gradually whisk in the Muscat and place the bowl over the pan of hot water. Whisk constantly for about 15 minutes or until the mixture thickens and increases to about 4 times it's original volume and is firm and frothy. Remove from heat.

Divide apples between 6 individual serving dishes and spoon over the warm zabaione. Serve immediately.

PANNA COTTA & PERE COTTE

Milk Custard (Osteria di via Solata) & Pears Baked in Red Wine (Chez Pierre)

Milk Custard

This classic Italian custard is the perfect comfort food and utterly soothing after a rich meal. Be sure to whisk the mixture constantly when cooking in order to avoid curdling. ⏱

Six 1$^1/_2$ g sheets unflavored gelatin
$^1/_2$ cup (125 ml) milk at room temperature
1$^2/_3$ cups (415 ml) cream
$^2/_3$ cup (165 g) white sugar
2 teaspoons vanilla essence
$^1/_2$ cup (125 ml) very strong espresso

Soften the gelatin sheets in the milk.

For the picture of Baked Pears in Red Wine, see page 109.

Pour the cream into a medium saucepan. Add the sugar and vanilla. Place over low heat and whisk constantly as the mixture comes to a boil. As soon as it boils, add the gelatin sheets and milk. Continue cooking, whisking constantly, for 1 minute.

Remove mixture from heat and add espresso. Pour into a medium bowl and place in a bain marie of iced water. Whisk for 15 minutes or until the mixture starts to thicken slightly. Divide between four 8 fl oz (250 ml) capacity molds and refrigerate until ready to serve.

Baked Pears in Red Wine

6 large hard, rough-skinned pears, peeled with stalks intact
2$^1/_4$ cups (570 ml) red wine
$^1/_2$ cup (110 g) sugar
2 whole cinnamon sticks
1 vanilla pod (optional)

Preheat oven to 250°F (130°C, gas mark 1/2).

Place the pears in an oven-proof dish and set aside. In a saucepan, bring the wine, sugar, and cinnamon to a boil. Add the vanilla pod (if using), then pour over the pears. Cover the dish and bake for about 3 hours, turning the pears halfway. Check for doneness with a skewer or fork, about 1 to 2 hours, depending on ripeness. Transfer the pears to a serving bowl to cool, and pour the liquid back into a saucepan. Discard the vanilla pod. Remove the cinnamon stick and set aside to garnish or discard.

Bring to a boil, stirring, until the liquid thickens to a syrup. Pour the syrup over the pears and baste well. Place pears in the refrigerator to chill thoroughly before serving. Garnish with cinnamon stick if desired.

"BONET" AL CIOCCOLATO E AL CAFFÈ

Chocolate Bonet and Coffee Bonet (La Contea)

Chocolate Bonet ⏱

3³/₄ cups (940 ml) milk
³/₄ cup unsweetened cocoa powder
10 eggs
1 cup (250 g) white sugar
5 oz (150 g) amaretto cookies, crumbled

Preheat oven to 325˚F (170˚C, gas mark 3).

Heat milk in a medium saucepan until almost boiling. Combine cocoa powder and ¹/₄ cup (60 ml) of the warmed milk in a small bowl until cocoa is dissolved. Place eggs and ²/₃ cup (165 g) of the sugar in a large bowl and whisk until sugar is dissolved. Slowly stir in the remaining milk, cocoa powder mixture and cookie crumbs until well-combined.

Place remaining ¹/₃ cup (85 g) sugar in a small saucepan with 1 tablespoon water over low heat. Stir constantly with a wooden spoon until it just begins to color. Pour into a warmed 14-cup (3¹/₂-liter) capacity pudding mold and twist the mold around so the toffee coats the bottom and sides. Set aside to cool. Pour the chocolate mixture into the mold and place in a deep baking pan with enough hot water to reach about 2 in (5 cm) below the rim of the mold. Bake in preheated oven for 1 hour or until a knife inserted into the center of the pudding comes out almost clean. Remove from oven and remove mold from bain-marie. Cool, then refrigerate several hours before serving. Serves 6 to 8.

Coffee Bonet ⏱

4 tablespoons white sugar
6 eggs
¹/₃ cup (85 g) white sugar, extra
1²/₃ cups (415 ml) cream
¹/₂ cup (125 ml) strong espresso coffee

Preheat oven to 325˚F (170˚C, gas mark 3).

Place 4 tablespoons sugar in a small saucepan with 1 tablespoon water over low heat. Stir constantly with a wooden spoon until it just begins to color. Pour into a warmed 14-cup (3¹/₂ -liter) capacity pudding mold and twist the mold around so the toffee coats the bottom and sides. Set aside to cool.

Separate eggs; place whites in a large bowl. Whisk until they form stiff peaks. Place yolks with the extra sugar into a large bowl and whisk until sugar is dissolved and mixture is a light yellow colour. Gradually stir in the cream and coffee until well combined. Gently fold half of the whisked egg whites into the cream mixture and, when just combined, gently fold in remaining cream mixture. Gently pour the coffee mixture into the mold and continue as for baking chocolate bonet (see above).

ZUPPA INGLESE

Italian-style English Trifle

⊘⊘⊘

6½ x 8 in (16 x 19½ cm) sponge cake, cut
 into ¼-in (½-in) thick slices (page 38)
1–2 tablespoons Alchermes liqueur, substitute
 with Marsala
1 tablespoon rum, diluted with 1 tablespoon
 cold water
2 cups (500 ml) milk
1 vanilla bean
3 eggs, separated
½ cup (125 g) white sugar
¾ cup (190 g) white sugar, extra
⅓ cup (85 g) all-purpose (plain) flour, sifted
Pinch salt
3 tablespoons candied fruit, finely chopped
1 tablespoon candied orange peel strips

Preheat oven to 400˚F (200˚C, gas mark 6).

Divide the sponge cake slices between two plates and sprinkle one lot with Alchermes (or Marsala) and the other with rum.

To prepare the pastry cream, place milk and vanilla bean in a small saucepan and bring to a boil. Remove from the heat, cover and infuse for about 15 minutes. Remove and discard vanilla bean.

Place egg yolks and sugar in a medium saucepan and beat until light and creamy. Continue beating while adding the flour and salt. Mix constantly with a wooden spoon while adding the milk in a thin stream. Place the saucepan over low heat and cook, stirring constantly and without allowing the mixture to come to a boil, until thickened. Strain the pastry cream into a small bowl. Carefully press a sheet of baking paper onto the surface of the pastry cream to prevent a skin from forming, and set aside to cool.

Reserve 3 tablespoons pastry cream. Pour the remaining pastry cream into a medium bowl and fold in the candied fruit.

Cover the base of an 8-in (20-cm) glass pie plate with the reserved 3 tablespoons pastry cream and arrange the sponge cake slices moistened with the Alchermes in the bottom. Top with the pastry cream mixed with candied fruit. On top of the pastry cream arrange the sponge cake moistened with rum to form a dome.

Whip the reserved egg whites to form soft peaks then gradually whisk in extra sugar, reserving 2 tablespoons. Whip until firm peaks form and the mixture is very thick. Cover the top of the dome with the meringue mixture and smooth the surface with a moist knife blade. Decorate with orange peel and sprinkle with reserved sugar.

Bake in preheated oven for 5 to 10 minutes or until the meringue is dry to the touch and lightly browned. Remove from oven and allow to cool completely before serving. Serves 6 to 8.

MONTE BIANCO

Chestnut Purée with Whipped Cream

This dessert gets its name from the tallest mountain in the Alps, Monte Bianco (Mont Blanc), and, when complete, it does resemble a lovely snow-covered mountain. The photo opposite shows the "neater"-looking version usually sold in shops. ⏱

1 lb (500 g) fresh chestnuts
2¹/₂ cups (625 ml) milk
¹/₃ cup (85 ml) milk, extra
²/₃ cup (85 g) white sugar
1 teaspoon vanilla essence
1 cup (250 ml) cream
2 tablespoons confectioners' (icing) sugar, sifted

Place the chestnuts into a medium saucepan with enough water to cover and place over high heat. Bring to the boil and cook for 10 to 12 minutes or until chestnuts skins are softened. Drain and remove outer and inner skins with a small knife whilst warm. Return to saucepan with the milk adding a little water if not enough liquid to cover. Place over medium heat and cook for 10 to 12 minutes or until quite tender. Drain chestnuts and crush them lightly with the back of a knife.

Return the chestnuts to the saucepan and add the extra milk, sugar, and the vanilla. Stir and bring to a boil. Cook for 10 minutes, stirring constantly, until the chestnuts have absorbed the milk and turned into a solid, homogenous mixture. Remove from heat and set aside.

Meanwhile, whip cream and confectioner's sugar until firm peaks are formed.

While chestnut mixture isstill warm, pass it through a potato ricer or sieve with large holes. Force it through the holes using the back of a wooden spoon or plastic spatula and onto a round serving platter. Move the ricer or sieve in concentric circles to shape the falling purée into a dome. Using a plastic spatula, cover the chestnuts with the whipped cream and smooth the surface with the blade of a knife. Serve immediately. Serves 4 to 6.

FRITTO MISTO ALLA PIEMONTESE

Piedmont-style Assorted Fried Meat and Vegetables (Il Cambio)

For the picture of Piedmont-style Assorted Fried Meat and Vegetables, see page 4.

4 eggs
1¼ cups (160 g) all-purpose (plain) flour
1½ cups (70 g) breadcrumbs
3½ oz (100 g) pork fillet
3½ oz (100 g) rump roast
3 oz (90 g) spinal marrow (optional)
3½ oz (100 g) calf's liver
3½ oz (100 g) veal thigh
3½ oz (100 g) veal fillet
4 lamb chops, about 12 oz (360 g) each
1 small chicken breast, about 5 oz (150 g),
    cut into 2/3-in (1½-cm) thick slices
5 oz (150 g) brains, cut into 4 equal pieces
1 large baby eggplant (aubergine), 3½ oz
    (100 g), cut into thin rounds
1 medium zucchini (courgette), sliced
4 fresh or frozen porcini mushroom caps,
    cut into 1/2-in (1-cm) thick slices
2 semolina cakes (1 regular, 1 chocolate),
    each cut into 8 equal pieces
1/2 cup (125 ml) cold milk
4 cups (1 liter) extra-virgin olive oil
8 amaretto cookies
1 large Red Delicious apple, peeled, cored,
    and cut into 2/3-in (1½-cm) thick slices
4 medium beef or pork sausages, cut in halves
Confectioners' (icing) sugar to taste
Salt to taste

In a large bowl, beat 2 of the eggs. Place 3/4 cup (95 g) of the flour on a plate. Place breadcrumbs on another plate. Cut the pork fillet, rump roast, and spinal marrow into 2/3-in (1½-cm) thick slices, and the liver, veal thigh and fillet into 1/2-in (1-cm) thick slices. Dust the lamb chops, chicken breast, pork fillet, rump roast, calf's liver, veal thigh, veal fillet, brains, marrow, eggplant, zucchini, mushroom caps, and semolina cake first in the flour, then in the eggs, and then in the breadcrumbs and set aside.

To make the batter, separate the remaining 2 eggs. Beat whites until quite stiff. In a large bowl, lightly beat the yolks. Add the remaining flour and the milk and mix well. Gently fold in the beaten egg whites.

In a large, heavy-based saucepan, heat 3 cups (750 ml) of the oil over medium heat. Dip the amaretto cookies, apple slices, and semolina cake in the batter and fry each separately until browned. Remove with a slotted spoon and transfer to paper towels. Keep warm. Skim oil and fry the remaining ingredients, separately, in this order: sausage, lamb chops, chicken breast, pork fillet, rump roast, calf's liver, veal thigh, veal fillet, brains, marrow, eggplant, zucchini, and mushroom caps. Add a little more oil if necessary. Arrange the fried amaretto cookies, apple slices, and semolina on a warm serving platter and sprinkle with sugar. Arrange the remaining ingredients and season all but the sausage to taste with salt. Serves 4 to 6.

INDEX

INDEX

PERIPLUS WORLD COOKBOOKS

TRAVEL THE WORLD IN YOUR KITCHEN!

Welcome to the world's best-selling international cookery series—and the first comprehensive encyclopaedia of world cooking! Each volume contains over 70 easy-to-follow recipes gathered in the country of origin. Introductory essays by noted food writers explore the cuisine's cultural roots and all food photographs are taken on location to ensure absolute authenticity. Truly the ultimate cookbooks for globetrotting gourmets!

"The scope of this library of books transcends the size of its volumes...They are thoughtful, well-planned, well-edited, and most importantly they strive mightily for authenticity, an effort sadly lacking in so many of today's 'ethnic' cookery books."

– "A Gourmet At Large" *Gourmet Magazine, USA*

The Food of Australia
ISBN 962 593 393 X Hardcover

The Food of Bali
ISBN 962 593 385 9 Hardcover

The Food of Jamaica
ISBN 962 593 228 3 Hardcover

The Food of Japan
ISBN 962 593 392 1 Hardcover

The Food of North Italy
ISBN 962 593 505 3 Hardcover

The Food of Paris
ISBN 962 593 991 1 Hardcover

The Food of Sante Fe
ISBN 962 593 229 1 Hardcover

The Food of Texas
ISBN 962 593 534 7 Hardcover